UNION OF SOVIET SOCIALIST REPUBLICS

PLACES AND PEOPLES OF THE WORLD

UNION OF SOVIET SOCIALIST REPUBLICS

Vincent V. DeSomma

CHELSEA HOUSE PUBLISHERS
New York   Philadelphia

COVER: The Cathedral of the Intercession (Cathedral of St. Basil the Blessed) is the oldest building in Moscow's Red Square. The cathedral—a complex of nine churches, each of which is crowned by an onion-shaped dome in different colors—was built for Ivan the Terrible in 1555–60.

FRONTISPIECE: In Moscow's Red Square, Soviet schoolgirls watch the changing of the guard at Lenin's tomb beside the Kremlin wall.

Chelsea House Publishers
Editor-in-Chief: Remmel Nunn
Managing Editor: Karyn Gullen Browne
Copy Chief: Juliann Barbato
Picture Editor: Adrian G. Allen
Art Director: Maria Epes
Deputy Copy Chief: Mark Rifkin
Assistant Art Director: Noreen Romano
Manufacturing Manager: Gerald Levine
Systems Manager: Lindsey Ottman
Production Manager: Joseph Romano
Production Coordinator: Marie Claire Cebrián

Places and Peoples of the World
Senior Editor: Kathy Kuhtz

Staff for UNION OF SOVIET SOCIALIST REPUBLICS
Copy Editor: Laurie Kahn
Picture Researcher: Patricia Burns
Designer: Robert Yaffe

First Printing

1 3 5 7 9 8 6 4 2

Library of Congress Cataloging-in-Publication Data
DeSomma, Vincent V.
Union of Soviet Socialist Republics/Vincent V. DeSomma.
p. cm.—(Places and peoples of the world)
Includes index.
Summary: Examines the history, geography, and society of the Soviet Union.
1. Soviet Union—Juvenile literature. [1. Soviet Union.] I. Title. II. Series.
DK41.D47 1991 90-21543
947—dc20 CIP AC
ISBN 0-7910-1370-7

CONTENTS

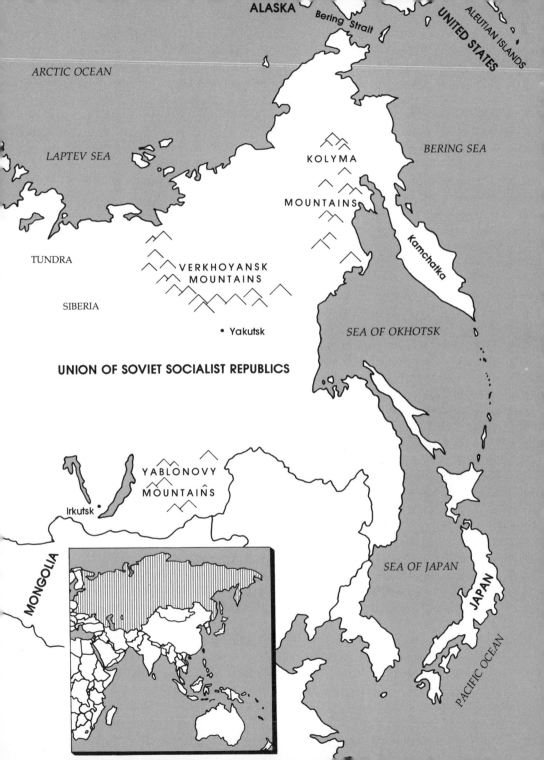

FACTS AT A GLANCE

Land and People

Area	8,649,538 square miles (22,402,303 square kilometers)
Population	284.5 million
Capital	Moscow (population 8,815,000)
Languages	Russian, 112 others
Major Cities	Leningrad, Kiev, Volgograd, Irkutsk, Vladivostok, Minsk
Major Rivers	Volga, Dnieper, Don
Religions	Christianity, Islam, Judaism, Buddhism
Major Ethnic Groups	Russian, Georgian, Ukrainian
Major Mountain Ranges	Ural, Verkhoyansk, Valdai Hills
Inland Seas	Black, Aral
Major National Holidays	May 1, Labor Day; November 7–8, October Revolution Day; December 5, Constitution Day

Neighboring Countries	Poland, Czechoslovakia, Hungary, Romania, Turkey, Canada, Japan, United States, Iran, Afghanistan, China, Mongolia
Number of Time Zones	11

Economy

Natural Resources	Gold, oil, natural gas, timber
Chief Exports	Automobiles, aircraft, natural gas, heavy machinery, vodka, caviar, military arms
Chief Imports	Technology, consumer goods, selected foodstuffs
Currency	Ruble (nonconvertible)

Government

Form of Government	Federal union (15 republics)
Head of State	President, elected by national legislature
Head of Government	Prime minister, appointed by president
Legislative Body	Supreme Soviet
Head of Communist Party	General secretary, elected by Central Committee

HISTORY AT A GLANCE

700 B.C.   The Slavs emerge as a distinct group.

A.D. 780   The Rus Varangians capture all of the Crimea, ruling their empire from Kiev on the Dnieper River.

856   Rurik seizes control of Rus with the aid of his brothers. He dies in 873. Rurik's successors, Oleg and Igor, wage war against the Byzantine Empire.

1054   The Tatars invade and by 1240 have conquered all of Russia. Their reign is marked by extreme brutality.

1147   Trader Yuri Dolgoruky establishes a *krmyl*, or post, on the Moscow River called Moscow and builds the first wooden Kremlin (fortress) in 1156.

1549   Russia's first Zemsky Sobor convenes. Composed of boyars, it elects Ivan IV the first czar, meaning "little father."

1613   The boyars elect 17-year-old Prince Michael Fedorovich Romanov as czar, thus ending the Time of Troubles. The Romanov dynasty is established.

11

1682–1725	Czar Peter I reigns. Deeply influenced by the West, he attempts to transform his backward country into a modern state, and largely succeeds.
1762–96	Czarina Catherine II reigns. She pursues some reforms and makes Russia a European empire.
1812–14	Napoléon Bonaparte of France invades Russia. He conquers Moscow and nearly topples the Romanov dynasty. Napoléon is eventually defeated, and Aleksandr I enters Paris as victor.
December 1, 1825	Aleksandr I dies, sparking the Decembrist uprising. It is squelched by his reluctant successor, Nicholas I.
March 3, 1861	The serfs are emancipated under Aleksandr II.
1894	Nicholas II assumes the throne at a time of great internal unrest.
1905	Popular uprisings are crushed by the regime. It is the first serious threat to the dynasty since Napoléon's invasion.
February 8, 1917	Revolution sweeps the capital, renamed Petrograd, but Nicholas II suppresses the uprising two days later. The *Duma* refuses to disband, and a provisional government is formed.
March 15, 1917	Nicholas II abdicates in his own name and that of his son, Alexis. Grand Duke Michael refuses the crown. The Romanov dynasty is ended.
October 7, 1917	Bolshevik forces seize Petrograd as the provisional government under Aleksandr Kerensky flees. Civil war begins.
1922	The Union of Soviet Socialist Republics is founded.
July 6, 1923	The first Soviet constitution is adopted.
January 21, 1924	Lenin, founder of the Soviet Union, dies. Joseph Stalin emerges as leader.

1936	A series of show trials begin against the "Old Bolsheviks." The Great Purge is launched.
December 5, 1936	A new constitution is adopted.
August 23, 1939	The Soviet Union and Nazi Germany sign a pact of nonaggression. It provides for the division of Poland and Soviet annexation of the Baltic states.
1939–40	The Soviet Union invades and defeats Finland, which had won its freedom from Russia after World War I.
June 22, 1941	Nazi Germany invades Russia, destroying the entire Soviet air force within hours.
1949	The Soviet Union detonates an atomic bomb, making it the second country after the United States to possess the weapon.
March 5, 1953	Joseph Stalin dies and is succeeded by Nikita Khrushchev.
1956	The Soviets suppress a popular uprising in Hungary.
1961	Soviet cosmonaut Yury Gagarin becomes the first man in space.
1964	Nikita Khrushchev is ousted from office and replaced by Leonid Brezhnev.
1968	Warsaw Pact troops crush a popular uprising in Czechoslovakia.
1972	U.S. president Richard M. Nixon visits the Soviet Union. The era of détente begins.
1977	A new constitution is adopted.
1979	The Soviet Union invades Afghanistan to prop up the pro-Soviet regime. Détente ends.
1980–85	Brezhnev dies and is succeeded by Yuri Andropov, who is succeeded by Konstantin Chernenko, both of whom die shortly after

taking office. Mikhail Gorbachev is elected Soviet leader.

1989 A new popularly elected legislature is formed, giving the people their first opportunity to democratically elect representatives. Reform sweeps society as the Communist party loses almost all credibility. The Communist regimes of Eastern Europe collapse.

January 1990 The Communist party relinquishes its monopoly on power, and a new government is formed with a powerful presidency.

July 1, 1990 The Soviets agree to the inclusion of a reunited Germany in NATO.

August 2, 1990 Iraq invades Kuwait. With Soviet cooperation, the UN Security Council condemns the invasion and later votes on economic sanctions against Iraq. That fall, an allied military coalition forms in the Persian Gulf region. The Soviet Union offers token assistance.

December 20, 1990 Foreign Minister Eduard Shevardnadze, Gorbachev's longtime ally, resigns.

January 13, 1991 Soviet army attacks unarmed nationalists in Vilnius, Lithuania, killing 15 people.

January 15, 1991 Deadline for Iraq to withdraw from Kuwait, as stipulated in UN resolution, which was supported by the Soviet Union.

January 16, 1991 United States and allies begin war with Iraq after UN deadline expires and no Iraqi withdrawal has occurred.

January 21, 1991 Soviet army continues its crackdown on the independence movement in the Baltics by laying siege to the Latvian government ministry building in Riga. At least five people are killed.

January 26, 1991 Gorbachev grants KGB extreme powers of search and seizure.

February 21, 1991   Gorbachev and his advisers announce to the UN coalition that they have put together a new peace plan with Iraq.

February 23, 1991   Ground assault by UN forces begins after Iraqi president Saddam Hussein misses deadline for pulling his troops out of Kuwait.

February 28, 1991   Cease-fire between Iraqi and UN forces is declared.

March 10, 1991   More than 150,000 Soviets march through Moscow demanding President Gorbachev's resignation.

March 17, 1991   National referendum is held to get the Soviet people's opinion on maintaining the Soviet Union as it now exists—that is, as equal, sovereign republics. Armenia, Estonia, Georgia, Latvia, Lithuania, and Moldavia officially boycott the vote, but the majority of the votes in the remaining republics support Gorbachev's union referendum.

In September 1989, in the republic of Azerbaijan, tens of thousands of Azeri nationalists defy Kremlin warnings and gather near a giant statue of Lenin in the main square in Baku, shortly before President Mikhail Gorbachev announced extensive reforms. The Soviet Union is composed of 15 republics and includes more than 100 nationalities.

1

The Soviet Union and the World

The largest country in the world is a multiethnic empire covering 11 time zones, stretching from Europe in the west to the Pacific Ocean in the east, from the Arctic Circle in the north to the craggy mountains of Central Asia in the south. With a population of 284.5 million, it is a military and political Goliath that has shared the title of "superpower" with the United States since 1945. And it is a deeply troubled country whose mounting problems affect virtually every corner of the globe. Few countries in history have had such vast influence for such a variety of reasons, which is why the Soviet Union is now one of the world's most important powers.

The Union of Soviet Socialist Republics (USSR), as it has been formally known since 1922, was created in 1917 by Lenin and the Bolsheviks, later called the Soviets, from the ashes of Imperial Russia. They shook the world by brutally instituting the first Communist state. Lenin and his successors, however, are only the most recent rulers of a land whose recorded history stems back to A.D. 150. Throughout the centuries and through many changes,

17

Russia has been a land of contrasts—rich and poor, czar and serf, artist and warrior. Ironically, the Soviet Union, which was created to eliminate those contrasts, retains many of the fundamental elements of Russian society.

Long a closed country, removed physically and culturally from the rest of the world, czarist Russia grew in every direction. The 19th century, in particular, witnessed the rapid expansion of the empire, which acquired, among other regions, all of Siberia. Today the Soviet Union consists of 15 republics: the Russian Federation, with its 16 autonomous regions; the Ukraine; Kazakhstan; Uzbekistan; Belorussia; Georgia; Azerbaijan; Moldavia; Lithuania; Latvia; Kirghizstan; Tadzhikistan; Armenia; Turkmenistan; and Estonia. They are home to more than 100 national groups.

The international community has always recognized Russia as a major power, yet Russia has rarely been seen as a true equal. The French, British, and Germans of the pre-20th century, who believed themselves to be the standard-bearers of Western civilization, considered the Russians neither European nor Asian—and always somehow inferior. Despite producing great writers and composers, such as Fyodor Dostoyevski and Pyotr Tchaikovsky, Imperial Russia felt compelled to import artisans from Italy and shipbuilders from Holland. This helped to instill western Europeans with a generally low regard for their neighbors to the east. The Russian reaction to such real and perceived slights, their persistent desire for military security, and an unwillingness to adopt 19th-century political liberalism further ingrained in their critics a mutual hostility that lingers to this day.

The Soviet Union has remained at the center of world attention throughout the 20th century. After the Revolution of 1917, international tensions increased dramatically as the new Soviet state set out to overturn the world order through the ideology of communism. Since the end of the World War II in 1945, the Soviet Union has played an even greater global role. Already a major

Asian power, the Soviet Union greatly expanded its influence after the war, first in Eastern Europe through the establishment of Communist governments under direct Soviet control—such as in East Germany, Czechoslovakia, Poland, Romania, Bulgaria, and Hungary—and later by supporting pro-Soviet rebel groups throughout the Third World, from the Caribbean to Africa to Asia. It also grew into a world-class military power. The Soviet Union's nuclear force, in particular, endowed the country with the capability to destroy the world and, with the United States, the ability to bring global peace.

Today the Soviet Union continues to fascinate the international community not only because of its strengths but because of the incredible changes taking place within the nation itself. In 1985, a fairly obscure junior member of the Politburo, the ruling council of the country, emerged as the leader of the Soviet Union. Mikhail Gorbachev—young, educated, and open—set out, slowly at first,

On June 1, 1990, President Mikhail Gorbachev (left) and U.S. president George Bush smile after signing several agreements, one of which expanded trade between the two countries. Gorbachev's policies of perestroika *and* glasnost *have helped to establish a new relationship with the West.*

to reform a country he perceived as growing increasingly weak. The Soviet people, proud of their heritage but intimidated by centuries of heavy-handed rule, were, in Gorbachev's mind, ready to revitalize their country economically and politically if only encouraged to do so. He instituted an economic policy known as *perestroika*, or "restructuring," and a social liberalization policy known as *glasnost*, or "openness." He also established new relationships with the Soviet Union's traditional adversaries—the United States, Western Europe, and China. The Soviet Union has not been the same since, and the world recognized Gorbachev's efforts abroad by awarding him the 1990 Nobel Peace Prize.

President Gorbachev's reform movement has been a mixed blessing for the Soviet Union. People may now speak their mind, free to criticize the government, the Communist party, and society in general. Not long ago, such expressions of opinion would have brought official harassment, arrest, and/or imprisonment. Artists and writers may now express themselves as they wish; newspapers may print the truth as it is, not as the government wishes it to be; and the faithful may openly practice their religion without

An American vendor from the state of New Jersey eats a slice of pizza near his pizza stand in Moscow in 1988. President Gorbachev's reform movement has encouraged foreigners to set up businesses in the USSR.

fear of persecution. It is a new experience for the peoples of the Soviet Union, and most have welcomed their new freedoms with gusto.

Much to the reformers' amazement, these changes have also placed the very future of the Soviet Union in doubt. By late 1989, the Soviet-allied Communist regimes of Eastern Europe—Poland, Hungary, Czechoslovakia, East Germany, Bulgaria, and Romania—had collapsed under the weight of public outrage, denying the Soviet Union its western empire. Many of the ethnic groups living within the Soviet Union itself have violently lashed out at their Russian rulers and one another; several republics, most notably the three Baltic states—Estonia, Latvia, and Lithuania—have declared a degree of independence from the Kremlin; and the Communist party is becoming increasingly subordinate.

The Soviet Union may well survive these turbulent times, to be reborn as an open, modern country embraced by the community of nations. Or it may crumble as it was born, amid chaos and violence. Whatever the future brings, the world community continues to watch as one of its giants gropes to find its way, for the Soviet Union's fate will affect the world well into the 21st century.

Peter the Great commissioned a French architect to build Peterhof (now Petrodvorets), his country palace, which is located near what is now Leningrad. The Grand Cascade, with its marble terraces, 3 waterfalls, and more than 64 fountains, has a waterworks system that dates from 1721.

2

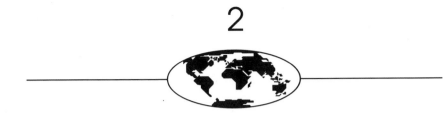

Geography and Wildlife

The Soviet Union, the largest country in the world, makes up one-sixth of the earth's land. It encompasses 8,649,538 square miles (22,402,303 square kilometers) and spreads over 170 degrees of longitude, dwarfing the world's second largest country, Canada, with its 3.8 million square miles (9,842,000 square kilometers). The USSR is bordered on the west by Poland, Czechoslovakia, Hungary, Romania, and Turkey; on the north by the Arctic Ocean; on the east by the Pacific Ocean; and on the south by Iran, Afghanistan, China, and Mongolia. This qualifies the Soviet Union as simultaneously European, Middle Eastern, and Asian.

The habitat of the Soviet Union consists of six different zones of soil and vegetation. Beginning in the north, they are the Tundra, the Northern Forest, the Forest Steppe, the Feather Steppe, the Semi-desert, and, far to the south, the Desert. These zones, which meld from one into the other, represent the very disparate geography that is Eurasia.

The Tundra, the northernmost zone, flat and bleak, stretches 4,000 miles (6,436 kilometers) across the country, from the Barents

Sea in the west to the Bering Sea in the east. It is a cold, uninhabitable region marked by low brush, bogs that freeze in the winter and fester in the summer, and permafrost—earth that is permanently frozen. The summer months are short and provide only a brief respite from the wind and cold that have made the Tundra one of the most inhospitable places on earth.

South of the barren stretches of the Tundra lies the Northern Forest. Although its perimeter is dotted with small clumps of thin trees and shrubs, the land gradually becomes a belt of thick, at times impenetrable, forest of birch, spruce, and pine. Called the taiga, this zone runs from northeastern Europe to the shores of the Pacific Ocean. The forest is so dense and the soil so poor that the area is best known for its hunting, trapping, and exportable timber harvests.

Farther south, the forests of the north are replaced almost entirely by Russia's famous birch trees. The flat Forest Steppe pro-

Tea leaves are harvested on a state farm in the republic of Georgia. Georgia, which shares part of its southern border with the Black Sea and which is crossed by the imposing Caucasus Mountains, is a land famous for its concentration of centenarians—people who are 100 years old or older.

duces perhaps as much as 85 percent of the world's birch. Because the trees are shallow rooted and the climate is considerably warmer than in the northern reaches, the soil is much better, though farming is not a major livelihood.

The Feather Steppe, to the south of the forests, is the Soviet Union's most important geographic area. Here the sparse trees are clumped together in groves, and between them are vast expanses of rich, flat land. This earth, mainly in the steppe's northern half, is ideal for farming, and it is here that the Soviet Union produces most of its grains—wheat, oat, barley, and rye. However, unlike the North American Midwest, the region sometimes receives little rainfall and can thus be an area of periodic famine.

Southward from the Feather Steppe the soil turns to hard rock and sand and is dotted by patches of brush. The temperature also begins to rise steadily. The Semi-desert may be of no agricultural use, but it does border the northern coast of the Black Sea, where Soviet citizens vacation—usually at their employers' expense.

East of the Black Sea the Semi-desert opens up into a true desert. The Desert is the southernmost reach of the Soviet Union and is primarily of strategic value. The sand and craggy hills of Central Asia give the Soviet military an eye to the south and the unsettled peoples and nations of the Middle East. That is why Imperial Russia made a point of conquering this otherwise unneeded wasteland.

The Rivers, Lakes, and Seas

There are more than 100,000 rivers running through the Soviet Union. The most famous are the Volga, 2,293 miles (3,689 kilometers) long, the Dnieper, 1,420 miles (2,285 kilometers) long, and the Don, 1,224 miles (1,969 kilometers) long. Because the landscape is so static, there is little change in the course of the rivers, though they are prone to flooding each spring, when the snows

The bazaar in Shakhrisabz, an ancient city in Uzbekistan, is frequented by tourists for its handicrafts, such as embossed copper, silk tapestry, and folk embroidery. Chorsu, a 15th-century covered market, can be seen at the far right.

melt in the north. Because of the general winter climate of the Soviet Union, only the rivers of Transcaucasia, in the southwest, flow year-round.

Many of the rivers flow to inland bodies of water, either to one of the thousands of lakes that are scattered across the country or to one of the Soviet Union's two landlocked seas, the Caspian and the Aral. The Caspian Sea, in particular, is enormous, covering more than 140,000 square miles (362,600 square kilometers). Though the water supply of the Soviet Union is extensive, it is also problematic. The freezing-and-thawing cycle between north and south results in ice jams and flooding, making regular passage of ships difficult throughout much of the year.

The Mountains

The mountain ranges that cross the Soviet Union include the Valdai Hills, located 200 miles northwest of Moscow, which are the source of the mighty Volga and Dnieper rivers. Far to the east are the Verkhoyansk Mountains of Siberia, which snake their way from the Laptev Sea in the north to the Mongolian border. The most important mountain range in the Soviet Union, however, is the Urals. The mineral-rich Ural Mountains divide European Russia from Siberia, and they remain the gateway to what most Soviets see as their "wild east." The Soviet Union is roughly divided into several regions. The best known is European Russia, stretching from the westernmost border with Eastern Europe to the Ural Mountains. This is where the bulk of the population lives and where most of the country's major cities—Moscow, Leningrad, Kiev, and Volgograd—are located. Moscow, the capital, is the largest, with a population of 8,815,000. European Russia is the home to Great Russians, Ukrainians, Latvians, Lithuanians, Estonians, and an assortment of smaller ethnic groups, including Poles, Germans, and Moldavians. To the south lies Transcaucasia, where a multitude of peoples live—often in harmony, frequently at odds. The region is most important to the Soviet Union because it is abundant in oil and other natural resources.

The largest region by far, however, is Siberia. Though completely conquered by the czars in the mid-19th century, Siberia has yet to be truly settled. Taken at face value, Siberia is a scarcely populated, barren wasteland in which a steady, biting wind is the only defining characteristic of its flat terrain of permafrost. For the czars, though, it was a route to a warm-water port on the open sea—the Pacific—and a convenient place to send political enemies and common criminals alike. In the past several decades, Soviet scientists have discovered large amounts of resources, such as natural gas, in the region, giving Siberia renewed importance.

Odessa's Potemkin Steps, the long stone stairway leading down to the Black Sea, were made famous in Sergey Eisenstein's epic film The Battleship Potemkin *(1925). In the climactic scene of the film, which is based on a mutiny during the 1905 Revolution, the czar's soldiers massacre innocent civilians as they descend the stairs.*

Climate

The climate of the Soviet Union is as varied as is its land. Because there are few mountain ranges to break the strong airflows that sweep down from the north and across Siberia, much of the country is exposed to frigid temperatures beginning as early as August and lasting into April. In Leningrad and Moscow, for instance, the average temperature in winter is no more than 7 degrees Fahrenheit (-14 degrees Celsius); it can be as cold as -47 ° F (-44° C) in Yakutsk, Siberia; and it is colder still near the Arctic Circle. In summer, temperatures in most major cities tend to be a bit more pleasant, averaging in the mid- to high 60s F (approximately 18°C), and reaching into the mid-80s F (30°C) farther south.

Participants prepare their reindeer for a race at the winter festival in Murmansk, the largest city inside the Arctic Circle. In this area of the far north, "night" lasts three weeks in the winter, and "day" lasts three weeks in the summer.

The average annual rainfall also varies across much of the country. For example, it rains 20 to 24 inches (51 to 61 centimeters) per year in European Russia, as little as 4 inches (10 centimeters) per year in the deserts of Central Asia, and as much as 40 to 60 inches (102 to 152 centimeters) per year in the mountains of the Pacific Coast.

Animal Life

Because the Soviet Union extends from the Arctic regions of the north to the parched subtropic lands of the south, the country boasts a fabulous array of animal life. Like the vegetation that becomes more plentiful toward the southern regions of the country, so, too, does the abundance of wildlife.

The Tundra is home to few animal species. Throughout the year, Arctic foxes and lemmings can be found scurrying about, and the occasional herd of reindeer can be spotted charging across the Tundra's hard, cold landscape. When the temperature is somewhat warmer in summer, numerous birds take to the air, including swans, long-tailed ducks, sandpipers, and geese. Moreover, the partially thawed earth releases swarms of gnats that blacken the air around pools of stagnant water.

Farther to the south, the Northern Forest springs forth with an abundance of wildlife. In the northern areas of the region are such beasts as the brown bear, the elk, and the coveted sable. Mouselike voles, wolverines, and lemmings also can be found. Among the many species of birds are the great gray owl, the woodpecker, and the bullfinch. Farther south in the forest, numerous deer, polecats, and nightingales can be seen. In the southernmost reaches of the region, many of the greatest and most fearsome creatures on earth reside: Black bears, leopards, and tigers stalk the thick woods, wary of no one but the hunters who also ply the dense terrain.

The animals of the steppes are at once plentiful yet constantly endangered. Such unique species as the marmot, jerboa, lark, and imperial eagle can be found in relative abundance. In the more eastern regions of the steppes, along the border with Mongolia, gazelle and pika roam freely. Unfortunately, the animal life of the region has been significantly altered over the centuries due to increased farming. The wild horse, for example, is now extinct, and many other species have migrated to find refuge in the forests of the north.

The most unusual animals of the Soviet Union can be found in the deserts of Central Asia. Whereas lynx, wildcat, jackal, and ass make the parched landscape their home, warbler, sand grouse, and jay soar on the dry winds above. As in any desert, a wide variety of lizards abound; arrow snakes slither, gray geckos sun themselves, and racer lizards speed along the parched landscape. Large numbers of bats prowl the night sky in search of insects.

The mountainous regions of the Soviet Union provide an assortment of exotic creatures that make higher elevations their home. The snow leopard, red deer, blue hare, goat, nutcracker, and woodpecker are found in the hills of Central Asia, and such diverse creatures as the suslik, partridge, and grouse flourish in the mountains of Siberia.

The country's extensive system of rivers, lakes, and seas holds a variety of fish life. Though the waters of the Arctic region are too cold to support many species, sturgeon, carp, and chub abound in the warmer waters of the Caspian, Black, Baltic, and Aral seas.

Its very size, diverse regions, and climactic extremes make the Soviet Union one of the most fascinating and important natural habitats in the world. It is for these reasons that environmental protection in the Soviet Union has become so important to everyone, Soviet and foreigner alike. Unfortunately, the Soviet government has, historically, fallen well behind its Western counterparts in working to protect endangered wildlife. In recent years, though, Soviet officials have made genuine strides toward preserving many of the species now in danger of extinction, such as the sable and sea otter. And as the Soviets continue to cooperate with the outside world, they will be able to improve their efforts to protect wildlife for future generations.

In 1916, the ballerina Anna Pavlova (1882–1931) poses for a photograph with another dancer. Pavlova enrolled at the Imperial Ballet School in St. Petersburg (now Leningrad) and later became well known for her interpretations of such classical roles as that in Giselle *and for her solo,* The Dying Swan.

3

Peoples and Cultures

The Soviet Union is the largest country on earth and is culturally one of the most complex. There are approximately 115 separate national groups and almost as many different languages within the borders of the Soviet Union. Many groups are culturally and/or linguistically linked, such as those of the western Slavic regions; others, such as the Asiatic peoples of Siberia, are unique within the Soviet mosaic. Together they constitute the very fabric of Soviet life, but their fundamental differences tug at the delicate weave that keeps the country intact.

The Soviet empire is a direct legacy of Imperial Russia, born of conquest and maintained through a delicate combination of concession and physical threat. The empire, ruled earlier from St. Petersburg and now from Moscow, is, in fact, a Russian empire. The Soviet state, regardless of its professed internationalism, is very much a Russian regime, and its outlook is distinctly Russian. The strength of Moscow's rule essentially stems from the Russian Republic's political, economic, and demographic domination of the country. Throughout the history of the empire, the Russians, ethnically known as the Great Russians, have constituted a clear majority of the population. Russian, which uses the Cyrillic alphabet, is the Soviet Union's chief language.

Today the Russians find themselves in the unenviable position of constituting approximately 50 percent of the population, and that number is rapidly decreasing. Not only are Russian birthrates in significant decline; there is a sharp increase among the other peoples of the empire. In particular, the birthrate among the Muslim peoples in the southern regions is rapidly increasing. These factors will soon place the Russians in the minority, unavoidably calling into question the very legitimacy of Russian rule.

The Soviet Union has been undergoing numerous political, economic, and social changes over the past few years, but none will have a more profound impact on the country than the challenge to Russian domination. Almost all of the republics, including Lithuania, Latvia, Estonia, and Georgia, have declared either their independence from the central government or their limited sovereignty. The Soviet state has lost much of its political credibility for a number of reasons, and it is that loss of credibility that has

In the 1890s this Belorussian couple, Philip and Pauline Chonin, left Minsk and immigrated to the United States. After the assassination of Czar Aleksandr II in 1881 and the rise in violent outbursts against Jews, Russians began to seek a happier life in America. By 1910, approximately 90,000 Russians, many of whom were from Belorussia, were living in the United States.

given the non-Russians a vehicle for justifying their declarations of independence. But at the core remains the issue of Russian rule; in short, non-Russians no longer fear the central government.

The Soviets, like the Imperial Russians before them, have ruled their domestic domain by compromise, concession, and intimidation. When the union of Soviet states was founded, a central goal was to maintain the empire while appeasing the non-Russians. By constitutional law, each republic and autonomous region retains its own government, for the most part a smaller version of the central government in Moscow, and reserves the right to secede from the Union. Until the mid-1980s, the actual independence of the republics was only nominal. The regional and local Communist parties were dominated by Moscow, and each closely followed the national leadership's wishes. This political allegiance easily translated into economic cooperation, and Moscow's rigid central control dictated economic policy in even the smallest of

On June 18, 1990, in Leningrad, Patriarch Aleksy II of the Russian Orthodox church leads a Sunday service to reopen Issaski Church, which had been closed for more than 50 years. Although the Soviet state denies the existence of God, the government is now permitting open religious observance, religious education in schools, and church charity work.

enterprises. The positioning of Soviet troops in those regions sent the strong message that physical rebellion would never be tolerated.

The Soviet Union is officially atheist; that is, the state denies the existence of God. This has resulted in the closing of churches and the persecution of religiously active citizens. The Soviets, however, have never been politically naive, and Lenin and his successors unofficially permitted the practice of religion in many of the non-Russian regions. Islam, in particular, has remained a vibrant part of life for the Muslim peoples of Central Asia.

Food and Drink

The favored food and drink of the Soviet Union tends to vary among ethnic groups. The peoples of Far Asia, for example, rely heavily on fish as a staple because they live close to the sea. In European Russia, bread and potatoes constitute the main dietary staple. Generally, the Soviets are not noted for their cuisine. Main courses, such as meat dishes, tend to be heavy, often smothered in creamy sauces. Certain foods, however, are known throughout much of the world, such as black bread and borscht, a thick beet and cabbage soup topped with sour cream. Russian caviar—raw sturgeon eggs—has long been an expensive delicacy and remains one of the Soviet Union's leading exports.

Most meals are enjoyed with wine, but because Russian wine tends to be exceedingly sweet, it cannot compete with the more delicate products of France and Italy. Russian vodka, however, may be the most widely consumed beverage in the Soviet Union, and it is eagerly imported by the West. Unfortunately, vodka has also become the bane of a country steeped in alcoholism.

Western foods have only recently made an impact on the Soviet Union. As a result of increased trade with the West, fast-food chains such as McDonald's, Pizza Hut, and Ben & Jerry's Ice Cream have been able to introduce uniquely Western foods to the

Soviet people, first in Moscow but eventually in other major urban centers as well. They have proven to be very popular, though less for their taste than for their novelty.

The Arts

The cultural life and heritage of the Soviet Union's numerous ethnic groups are as different as the peoples themselves. Each culture has significantly added to the life of all the Soviet peoples, and each stands as unique in its own right. Georgian music and dance, for instance, are world renowned, and the Ukrainians' cossack heritage distinguishes them from their Soviet compatriots. (Descendants of fierce horseback warriors who exchanged their services for preferential treatment from the czars, the cossacks remain an independent force in the modern Soviet Union.)

It is Russia, though, that has made truly outstanding contributions to a broader intellectual life. When Peter the Great invited western European artisans to help build his new city of St. Petersburg, it was, in part, a reflection of the czar's personal prejudices. Indeed, it was during the Byzantine period (988–1530) that icon painting was born. Icons—religious images that adorned Russia's churches, palaces, and private homes—became as important a symbol of the devout religious beliefs of Russians as the cross itself. Later, the so-called Novgorod School introduced the magnificent frescoes that to this day make Russia's churches and former royal residences among the world's most beautiful structures.

The 18th and 19th centuries witnessed the influence of Western art on Russian artisans. The course of Russian art during this period had much to do with the individual tastes of the reigning czars and czarinas. French culture had a strong impact on many of Europe's royal houses, and the Russian royalty was not immune. Such Russian artists as Ivan Argunov and Fedor Rokotov, who studied under imported French masters, reflected this influence in their work. Events such as the Napoleonic invasion, however, reinstilled the arts with a sense of Russian nationalism, and subsequent painters, such as Ilya Repin (1844–1930), adopted uniquely Russian themes; Repin's *The Volga Bargemen* is probably the most popular painting of this period.

The late 19th century and the first years of the 20th century witnessed a strong Russian contribution to modern art. The shocking effects of modern art, such as Cubism, Expressionism, Constructivism, and Suprematism, were interpreted by many European traditionalists as an implicit endorsement of political radicalism; in reactionary Russia, modernists were persecuted. Indeed, ultramodernist artists such as Ilya Mashkov (1881–1944) and Aleksandr Kuprin (1870–1938) were, at the very least, intellectually sympathetic to the movements of the Left. The struggle between traditionalism and modernism in Russian art truly reflected the struggles in Russian political life.

Russia developed its own unique style of architecture as well. The history of Russian architecture can be broken into 4 principal periods—the Byzantine (10th to 16th century), the Muscovite (16th to 18th century), the European (18th to early 20th century), and the Soviet (early 20th century to present).

The Byzantine period reflected the styles of eastern Europe, most noticeably in the construction of churches. Russia's adoption of Eastern Orthodox Christianity during this period translated into its architecture. The Cathedral of St. Sophia, built in Kiev in 1037, for example, has undergone several changes but retains much of its original design, characteristic of those constructed earlier by the Greek Orthodox church. The most prominent characteristic of the Byzantine period is the use of onion-shaped domes. Most of these structures were built of wood because of the abundance of forests and thus have long since vanished.

The Muscovite period marked the emergence of a uniquely Russian form of architectural design. It was during this period that the two most recognizable Russian structures were raised—the Kremlin in Moscow and the Cathedral of St. Basil the Blessed (now called the Cathedral of the Intercession) outside its gates. The Kremlin was originally a walled wooden fortress used to protect traders in an untamed land. Between 1475 and 1510, Italian artisans were hired to create a more permanent Kremlin after the original had burned. Located in the middle of Moscow, the Kremlin contains three churches and several palaces. Once the home of the monarchy, the Kremlin is today the seat of the Soviet government. The Supreme Soviet and the offices of the Soviet Union's top officials are within its walls.

The Cathedral of St. Basil the Blessed, located at the far end of Red Square, which runs along one side of the Kremlin, was erected between 1555 and 1560. Fashioned in masonry after the style of the wooden churches of the Byzantine period, it is adorned in bright, contrasting colors and is one of the most visually spectacular structures in the world.

Within the redbrick walls of the Kremlin—the oldest section of Moscow—stand the Bell Tower of Ivan the Great (far right), the cathedrals of the Archangel and the Annunciation (center), and the Grand Kremlin Palace (left), among other buildings. The Grand Kremlin Palace, which was once the site for palaces of grand dukes and czars, is today the seat of the Supreme Soviet, the USSR's legislative body.

The European period reflected the czars' and czarinas' taste for the western European style of architecture. Such grandiose works as Peter I's Winter Palace in St. Petersburg, Catherine's Palace outside Moscow, and the Bolshoi Theater in Moscow are akin to the residences, government buildings, and public sites of their Western counterparts. Still, they retain a distinctly Russian flavor.

The Soviet period may be more accurately referred to as the Stalinist period. Under the reign of Joseph Stalin (1928–53) the Soviet state undertook enormous construction projects, in part to prove the success of the regime. Determined to break with the past, the Soviets adopted a style perceived as modern that was, in fact, cold and imposing. Seven "skyscrapers," for example, with their bulky towers and blank facades, dominate the Moscow skyline. In recent decades the Soviets have moved away from this approach and have begun to work with steel and glass, in a style similar to that of Western office buildings.

Musically, Russians have contributed to the arts in numerous ways. Perhaps the music most readily identified with Russia is produced by the balalaika. This six-stringed triangular instrument resembles a guitar but produces a tinnier sound, and even today at least one person who is proficient on the balalaika can be found in almost every Russian village.

Russia can claim many of classical music's leading figures as its own. Pyotr Tchaikovsky and Igor Stravinsky are universally recognized as two of the world's greatest composers, and their instrumental and operatic works continue to thrill audiences around the globe. Today, Soviet musicians continue that long tradition, and Soviet orchestras and opera companies are among the world's finest.

Russia's tradition of excellence in the field of ballet has been an inspiration to the world. The development of modern Russian ballet can be attributed to Sergey Diaghilev (1872–1929), who was known for introducing Western Europe to Russian culture at the

Composer Igor Stravinsky (left) and dancer-choreographer Vaslav Nijinsky collaborated on the ballet Pétrouchka *in 1911. The ballet, which was first performed by Nijinsky in Diaghilev's Ballets Russes, is the tragic story of a puppet endowed with a human heart.*

turn of the 20th century. He subsequently founded a Russian dance troupe, the Ballets Russes, in 1909 and within a few short years gained world acclaim. Upon his death in 1929, Diaghilev was succeeded by the choreographer George Balanchine (who later immigrated to the United States and established the American School of Ballet, now the New York City Ballet).

Russia's ballet schools, including the Bolshoi in Moscow and the Kirov in Leningrad, have consistently produced many of the world's greatest ballet dancers and choreographers. Lev Ivanov, Vaslav Nijinsky, Anna Pavlova, Rudolph Nureyev, and Mikhail Baryshnikov are but a handful of ballet geniuses who have come from the Russian ballet tradition.

The Soviet Union's world-renowned museums, such as the Hermitage in Leningrad, provide a vivid look into old Russia. Despite their concerted effort to break with the past, the Soviets have taken great care to preserve the relics of bygone eras. The trappings of the monarchy—gilded coaches, crown jewels, and elaborate vestments—dazzle museum visitors. Soviet museums also provide splendid showcases for the country's extensive collection of priceless artwork.

For those Soviets who prefer lighter entertainment, the circus provides a wonderful show. Skilled acrobats, dancing bears, clowns, and musicians continue to thrill audiences. The Moscow Circus, for example, regularly tours the world.

Literature and Theater

Few peoples have made as strong an impact with the written word as the Russians. Russian literature itself can be traced back to the 11th century. From then until the 18th century it possessed a strongly religious theme. As in most of Europe, those people outside the ruling nobility who were literate were religious leaders; understandably, they wrote about what they knew best. At roughly the same time, the Russian parable gained prominence. These light stories were, in fact, written to impart a meaning to everyday life and were easily understood and widely popular.

It was not until the 19th century, however, that Russian literature fully blossomed. Poetry in particular became an important literary form, and the Russian people's near devotion to verse

In July 1988, Soviet fans mob West German singer Udo Lindenberg (left) and Soviet singer Alla Pugachova (center) in a Moscow record shop, hoping to get the stars' autographs. Music from the West, such as rock and American jazz, is popular in the Soviet Union.

became universally recognized as a window into the Russian soul. Perhaps the greatest Russian poet was Aleksandr Pushkin (1799–1837). During his brief but rousing lifetime, Pushkin produced a long list of many of the world's finest poems, and works such as *Eugene Onegin*, a verse-novel about a shallow, pleasure-loving man's insensitivity toward the love of a noblewoman, which took seven years to complete, displayed a beauty and ability matched by few other poets. Pushkin's ability to capture human sympathy in his characters—most of whom are seen as victims rather than as judges of their own fate—has rarely been equaled.

The 19th century was also a heyday for Russian prose. The first great Russian writer of the modern era was Nikolay Gogol (1809–52), and it was he who set the standard for modern Russian literature. Gogol was both a novelist and dramatist, and his works were the first to serve as social commentary. His 1836 play *The Inspector General*, about a small town's reaction to a visiting dignitary, illustrated the absurdity of life under the czars through biting humor. Literature has always been an outlet for social frustrations, but in oppressive Russia it became even more so.

Fyodor Dostoyevski (1821–81) followed Gogol in expressing the inequities and injustices of Russian society through literature, but with a more somber tone. His novels *Crime and Punishment*, *The Possessed*, and *The Brothers Karamazov* sadly described not only the hopelessness and despair but the conditions of everyday Russian life and the negative impact that those conditions had on common thinking. In the 19th century, Dostoyevski was to Russia what Charles Dickens was to England.

The writings of Lev Tolstoy (1828–1910) also illuminated the plight of the common man, but Tolstoy did so through his portrayal of the individual, in novels such as *War and Peace* and *Anna Karénina*. He attempted to show how flaws of character led to the horrors of Russian life. Tolstoy's works were ultimately interpreted as more of an insight into human nature itself than a social

The writers Lev Tolstoy (left) and Maksim Gorky pose for a photograph in 1900. Tolstoy, who was born to a wealthy family, and Gorky, who was born to a working-class family, frequently wrote about moral issues and the suffering of the peasants. Both writers were controversial in their time—Tolstoy was excommunicated from the Russian Orthodox church in 1901 for his antireligious views and Gorky was exiled from Russia after the 1905 Revolution failed.

commentary. Nonetheless, no one can deny that Tolstoy was one of Russia's—and the world's—greatest literary figures.

Anton Chekhov (1860–1904) and Maksim Gorky (the pen name of Aleksey Peshkov, 1868–1936) best illustrate the very different strains in Russian literary life. Chekhov's numerous short stories and plays took a decidedly nonpolitical approach, and his works were hailed not as social commentary but as pure literature and drama. Chekhov was a medical doctor from a relatively prosperous Moscow family who harbored less social outrage than did many of his contemporaries. Gorky, on the other hand, came from a poor background and never forgot the chronic suffering of the peasant class. His plays and poems reflect his political radicalism, and the Soviets presumptuously hailed him as one of their own.

Social Life

Life in prerevolutionary Russia was an odd mix of uniquely Russian interests and practices and an active desire to be "Western." Prior to the 18th century, Russia had been a society effectively cut off from the West by distance and, as such, was at no other time as free from outside influences. The 200 years following, however, witnessed the Russian ruling classes' wish to adopt Western standards and practices. The desire to be accepted as an equal to the West pervades Russian thinking to this day.

The Russian merchant and industrial classes of the 18th and 19th centuries also viewed Western life as a cultural standard. Their children learned French, the "international" language, they eagerly awaited the latest fashions from Paris and London, and they sponsored artists who had adopted Western techniques. They traveled widely and, with their money, extended much of Western society to their corners of Russia. Each of Russia's major cities—Moscow, St. Petersburg, and Kiev—had a fashion district where nattily dressed men and women strolled the streets; schools were established to teach young ladies the finer points of high society; homes were decorated in Victorian style; elegant restaurants staffed French chefs; and orchestra and opera houses were built in the finest of traditions.

What these new "Westerners" did not bring with them was a broader sense of democracy; they believed that only through czarism could they safeguard their positions. Their adopted life-styles succeeded in drawing an even greater distinction between the few and the many and, in the process, succeeded in aggravating an already explosive situation.

Ivan IV, first czar of Russia, ruled from 1533 to 1584. Ivan's often merciless pursuit of national and personal aggrandizement earned him the name by which he is best known, Ivan the Terrible.

4

Prerevolutionary Russia

The first people known to have settled the vast lands that are now the Soviet Union were the Slavs. Because they left no written records behind, it is difficult to pinpoint precisely when they began to settle the region. But it is known that the Slavs were a distinct group by 700 B.C.

As they gained a more permanent foothold in the region and their numbers continued to grow, the Slavs spread out across the wide expanses at their disposal. One group moved westward into what is now Eastern Europe, another headed south into the Balkan mountains, and a third went east into the fertile steppes—they were the predecessors of the Russians and Ukrainians. A small offshoot of this last group, known as the Varangians, moved northward into the thick forests. Each group quickly adapted to its surroundings, either hunting, fishing, trapping, or farming, depending on the quality of the soil and the climate.

In time, the proliferation of different tribes eventually led to warfare and the establishment of recognized borders. The Varangians were the first to found a state, which they called Rus, making their capital in Kiev, on the Dnieper River. Soon the Rus

Varangians were expanding their territorial holdings and by A.D. 780 had seized all of the Crimea.

In 856 a warrior chief named Rurik emerged; with the aid of his brothers, he seized control of Rus and established a formal Kievan state. Rurik ruled Kiev for 17 years, until his death in 873, allowing his successor, Oleg, to assume control of the burgeoning kingdom. In 907, Oleg attacked Constantinople (the capital of the Byzantine Empire, known today as Istanbul), and his successor, Igor, struck the city again in 944. Kiev had become a credible power by A.D. 1000.

By 1054, however, power struggles and family feuds significantly weakened Rus to the point where it could effectively defend neither itself nor its trade routes. It was not surprising, then,

A 1628 woodcut of the plan of Moscow. Moscow, founded by Yuri Dolgoruky in 1147, lies between the rivers Volga and Oka, on the banks of the Moscow River (a tributary of the Oka). The word Kremlin, *which today refers to the governing center of the Soviet Union, is derived from the Russian word* krmyl, *the wooden fortress that surrounded the settlement.*

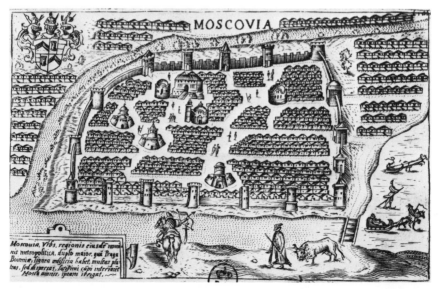

that by 1240 all of Russia would fall to the invading Tatars from the east. The Tatars ruled over their empire with brutality, and their reign left a deep impression on the Slavs. Not until 1480 would Russia again be free, but in 1147 a seemingly small event occurred that would eventually be of major importance to Russia: A trader by the name of Yuri Dolgoruky established a *krmyl*, or post, on the Moscow River, appropriately named Moscow. (The term *Kremlin*, which comes from the word *krmyl*, refers to the wooden fortress that Dolgoruky built around the settlement in 1156.)

Ivan III

Centrally located on several important trade routes, Moscow rapidly grew into a recognized center of commerce. After being sacked and burned in 1382, Moscow was liberated from the Tatars in 1480 by Prince Ivan III. It soon became the undisputed seat of power in the east. Ivan III, known as Ivan the Great, not only expanded the rule of Moscow through his control of massive armies; he also established the Russian Orthodox church. In 1439 the Greek Orthodox church, which claimed numerous followers across Russia, "unified" with the Roman Catholic church. This union was rejected by many Russians, who believed their crown prince to be the successor to the Byzantine emperors. Through adherence to his own faith and a ready willingness to forge a political bond between the Crown and Russia's religious leaders, Ivan the Great inextricably tied the new church to the throne.

Ivan the Terrible

It was not until 1547 that another grand prince, Ivan IV, took the first steps toward building a true kingdom. When Ivan IV assumed the throne at the age of 16, he inherited a loose federation of divergent ethnic groups. Under the influence of his most prominent subjects—especially those in business, government, and the church—the crown prince instantly recognized that if his rule was to last, he had to transform his domain into a politically unified kingdom. He did so through a combination of political maneuvering and sheer force.

In 1549, Russia's first *Zemsky Sobor*, or "the assembly of the country," convened. Composed of *boyars*, local princely landowners, the Sobor elected Ivan IV the first czar, which means "little father" in Russian. Ivan IV quickly used his new powers to further expand the country territorially, but in 1558 he sought a port on the Baltic, and, consequently, Russia suffered her first real defeat at the hands of the Poles. This blow, coupled with his insistence that he alone reserved the right to rule, put Ivan IV at odds with the boyars.

Instead of directly confronting his enemies, however, Ivan IV simply circumvented them. He divided all of the land in Russia between the monarchy and the boyars. He gave away much of the land that he had claimed for himself, thus creating a new landowning class that owed allegiance to the throne. Soon the traditional economy collapsed, and Ivan IV emerged as the unquestioned authority in Russia.

Ivan IV was one of the most influential figures in Russian history, but he was also one of the most feared. He was a creative ruler who devised the system of proportional taxation and used state funds to support the arts. He hired the country's finest artisans to adorn his palaces and churches with their icons and mosaics. Yet he was also a tyrant who would kill messengers for bringing bad news, level cities—such as Moscow's rival city, Novgorod—and kill many of their inhabitants, and in whose mere presence members of his court and family would shudder. For whatever good he may have done for Russia, Ivan IV may be best known for murdering his own son in a fit of rage, an act that he regretted for the remainder of his life.

By the end of Ivan IV's reign, Russia had become a land of contrasts. It was developing faster than had most other states, but it was also becoming increasingly oppressive. Indeed, life under Ivan IV became so difficult that refugees regularly fled across the borders to escape Ivan the Terrible. Perhaps the most distasteful development was the institution of serfdom. The boyars were small kings in their own right, and those who lived under them were at their beck and call. Although many peasants owned small plots of land, many worked on the boyars' vast estates. Heavily taxed, they were unable to pay what they owed their masters, so they continued to work, and debts continued to rise. The serfs were forbidden to leave the estates and so were forever in debt. Their indentured status soon became an institution, and an entire segment of the population in essence became slaves. This state of affairs would haunt Russia for the next two centuries.

The Romanovs

By the early 17th century, Russia had become a major regional power, a change that did not go unnoticed among its more stable neighbors to the west. On September 30, 1610, an invading Polish army entered Moscow, and except for a Russo-Polish treaty supported by the embittered boyars, Russia came perilously close to falling under direct Polish rule. Infighting ensued, and the next three years became known as the Time of Troubles.

In 1613, the boyars finally moved to resolve the lingering crisis: They elected a czar, a 17-year-old prince from among their ranks, Michael Fedorovich Romanov. Michael and his two immediate successors, Alexis and Fedor III, ruled Russia until 1682. Their successive reigns solidified the Romanov dynasty and in the process began to shape Russia the kingdom into Russia the nation. A nominal constitutional monarchy was adopted from the old Moscow state—rule divided between the Crown, the *Duma* (boyar's council), and the *Sobory* (local land councils). In fact, the dynasty gradually assumed almost complete control over the country— authority limited only by the sheer size of the kingdom.

The Russian Orthodox church also grew in stature; for from it extended the "divine" legitimacy of the throne. Within the church itself, however, a schism opened between reformers, led by Czar Fedor, and the so-called Old Believers, those who remained committed to the original practices of the church. In the long run, it was the Old Believers who most consistently supported the throne.

As a relatively powerful state, Russia under the first Romanovs began to take on regional stature. Peace treaties were signed with Poland and Sweden, Russia's historical adversaries. The czars ceded much of their territory in the north, but they were quick to move to the west and south whenever their neighbors appeared weak. At the same time, a small but growing community of for-

Peter I, called Peter the Great, was determined to make Russia equal to its neighbors in the West and transformed it from a backward country into a modern state. He established Russia as northern Europe's leading military power and founded a new capital, St. Petersburg, which gave Russia an outlet to the Baltic Sea.

eigners, mainly traders, established themselves in Moscow, and their influence grew steadily. By the mid-17th century, Russia was well on its way to becoming a true power, although it would not become a world-class empire until the 18th century.

Peter the Great

Between 1682 and 1725, Russia underwent a rapid transformation from a land of backward, inward-looking princes and peasants to an emerging political, financial, and military power recognized throughout Europe. This was due to the efforts of one man, Czar Peter I, who would be remembered forever as Peter the Great. A man of keen intellectual powers, Peter was unquestionably the premier authority in Russia, not only because he was the czar, but because his personality, determination, and frequent ruthlessness made him a difficult figure to resist.

Peter the Great's determination to transform his country derived largely from the fact that the young monarch had traveled widely in Europe. Unlike his predecessors, who cared little about how the world worked beyond Russia's borders, Peter yearned to see firsthand exactly what it was that made a great power great. So he set out for the cities of the West in disguise; after all, a czar would be treated as a dignitary, not a student. Peter's travels took him to many of Europe's great cities, including Amsterdam, London, and Prague. He saw marketplaces in action, civil servants at work, factories at full capacity, banking institutions in operation, and military machines fitted with modern weapons—and he was impressed.

Back home, Peter immediately set out to make Russia an extension of the West, whether or not his people liked it. Taxes were raised to construct a new capital on the marshy banks of the Baltic, aptly named St. Petersburg, and Italian artisans were brought in to make this "door to the West" a proud symbol of the new Russia.

Textile factories sprung up across the landscape, a civil service was created, and the government was divided into administrative departments. A senate was formed to replace the Duma. The military, especially the navy, was completely reorganized and refitted, which Peter used with particular effectiveness to significantly expand the empire's territorial possessions. The Russian Orthodox church was placed under the direct jurisdiction of the throne through the creation of the Holy Governing Synod, thus stripping the church of its independent authority. Military and technical academies were established as science and engineering began to flourish. And relations with the West were greatly expanded. Peter established formal diplomatic ties with such great powers as England and Holland and encouraged travel and trade between his empire and the developed world. Thanks to Peter the Great, Russia was thrust into the modern age.

The road to modernization under Peter I was by no means easy, and much of the czar's energy was spent on "convincing" his subjects that modernization was in the best interest of the kingdom. An absolute monarch need not use political persuasion to have his way, merely a forceful hand. Peter believed that if Russia was to be modern, then it must look modern—which was largely the rationale for building St. Petersburg. When members of his court, for example, refused to shave off their beards, as did Western noblemen, Peter did it for them. He was powerful but not always well liked, and by the end of his reign, Peter's Russia was plagued by regional unrest and peasant revolts. Nevertheless, history has recorded Peter I as one of its greatest figures.

Catherine the Great

If Peter I made Russia a modern nation, then it was Catherine II who made it a modern empire. Catherine, born Princess Sophia in Prussia in 1729, assumed the Russian throne in 1762 as the result of the often violent court intrigue—with the help of her sup-

Catherine II continued Peter I's drive to westernize Russia and add territories to the empire. During Catherine's reign, domestic reforms, such as rewriting the code of law, increased the efficiency of provincial administration and improved the nation's banking system. Catherine was also a great patron of musicians, artists, and philosophers of the Enlightenment movement.

porters, Catherine overthrew her husband, Peter III—but she quickly proved herself worthy of the title czarina.

After Peter I's death in 1725, it had become fashionable among his survivors to declare themselves modernizers in his mold, but few could match him either politically or intellectually. Catherine, however, was quite the opposite. A well-read woman who was widely versed in the liberal thinking of the day, Catherine set out to fashion an enlightened reign where rule of law dictated policy. She established a parliament representing a cross section of the empire and crafted a new legal code. Not surprisingly, the czarina met sharp resistance from the landowning class, which eventually pressured her into relinquishing much of her domestic authority.

She did establish a local system of government, though, that lasted well beyond her reign.

Frustrated by the sluggish pace of her reforms at home, Catherine turned her attention to foreign affairs. One of her principal objectives was the conquest and annexation of Russia's traditional enemy, Poland. Through a deft agreement with Prussia concluded in 1772, she managed to absorb the eastern half of that country, including the city of Warsaw. Catherine's goal of driving the Turks from the southern shore of the Black Sea failed despite two wars against the Ottoman Empire, but her overall success in the politics of alliance made Russia a full member of the European community.

Catherine may have gone down in history as an even greater reformer than her predecessor, Peter I, had it not been for developments at the other end of Europe. In 1789 popular revolution swept France, toppling one of the most powerful monarchies in the world. Perhaps it was the specter of a worldwide democratic movement (the Americans had freed themselves from British rule in 1783) or the news that King Louis XVI had been publicly beheaded; in any event, Catherine abandoned her reform movement, and whatever chance there might have been for a constitutional monarchy in Russia came to a screeching halt.

When she died in 1796, Catherine the Great left behind a mixed legacy. She had earned Imperial Russia a place among the most powerful countries and had introduced several enduring domestic reforms; but she failed to abolish serfdom and to give the kingdom a genuine constitutional system. Little did she know that she may well have set the stage for one of the greatest upheavals in modern history.

Aleksandr the Great

Aleksandr I, Catherine's grandson, was similar to his grandmother in several respects. Intelligent and worldly, the young

Aleksandr was Catherine's favorite if for no other reason than that her son—Aleksandr's father, Paul I—was a madman given to fits of rage. After Paul's assassination in 1801, liberal reform once again sprang from the czarist throne, and once again Russia was offered the chance to become a truly enlightened monarchy.

Aleksandr I and his private advisory committee, composed of his most trusted allies, set out to establish a permanent rule of law. Serfdom, still the most chronic problem in the realm, was quietly approached, and, in 1803, a royal *ukaz*, or edict, was issued giving landowners the right to free their serfs, though few did. A drive was begun to overhaul the educational system, and three new universities were established. But Aleksandr walked a tightrope between cautious reform and revolution. On one side he had the fiercely reactionary landowners and their church allies; on the other, committed constitutionalists and radicals. He could ill afford to move too far one way or the other.

With the Russian army in pursuit, Napoléon's Grand Army retreats from Russia in October 1812. Napoléon was forced to leave Russia when winter set in—thousands of his troops had been killed during the invasion, and those who were left were starving or freezing to death. Napoléon's invasion and defeat in Russia were later immortalized in Tolstoy's War and Peace.

Aleksandr might have gone down in history as yet another moderate czar had it not been for French emperor Napoléon Bonaparte's invasion of Russia in 1812. As Napoléon trampled across most of Europe, Aleksandr had tried first to ally Russia with France's enemies and later to ally it with Napoléon himself in an attempt to ward off a French attack. When Napoléon finally turned his massive armies against Russia, Aleksandr found himself swept up in a nationalist furor. Conservatives in Russia disapproved of the czar's ties to Paris and indirectly blamed Aleksandr for the French assault. He could now only foster the nationalism that would hopefully save his kingdom from French rule and his throne from the Russian nobles.

Napoléon's invasion of Russia was one of the most important and devastating events in modern history. French legions laid waste to everything in their path, destroying cities, ravaging crops, and killing thousands. It seemed as if the Russian monarchy were finished when Napoléon triumphantly marched into a burning Moscow and straight into the Kremlin, the czar's Moscow palace. But the freezing weather set in and Napoléon, who did not want to be isolated in Moscow over the winter, was defeated in 1814. Aleksandr rode into Paris at the head of his armies and into the councils of Europe. In the search for a more just world order, he created the Holy Alliance of enlightened monarchs. It made Aleksandr an international hero.

Aleksandr did not receive such wide affection at home. Many returning veterans, influenced by the liberalism of the West, tried to make Aleksandr live up to his promises of reform; proposed constitutions were soon being drawn up, and debating societies were being formed to promote the ideas of wholesale reform. The reaction from the ruling classes was swift and fierce, and between 1820 and 1825 the state launched a campaign to eliminate the liberal movement. School curricula were overhauled, revolution-

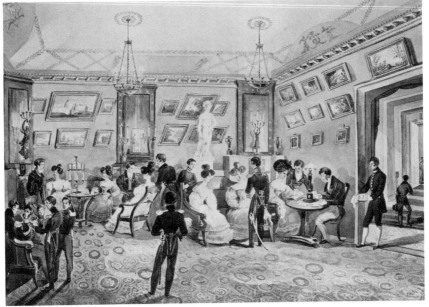

An 1830 watercolor depicts a gathering of aristocrats at a St. Petersburg salon. In December 1825, a group of patriotic, intelligent aristocrats revolted against Nicholas I. The Decembrists, as they were called, advocated a constitutional government, the abolition of serfdom, and the freedoms of the press, speech, and religion. Although they suffered a crushing defeat, they became a noble symbol to later Russian revolutionaries who fought against autocracy.

ary organizations were banned, and subversives were routed. The reign of Aleksandr I ended very differently than it had begun.

Nicholas I

Aleksandr I's unexpected death on December 1, 1825, brought the struggle between the reactionaries and the reformers to a bloody head. It was unclear who would succeed Aleksandr—the late czar's eldest brother, Constantine, or his younger brother, Nicholas. The former did not want the throne, and the latter did not know what to do. Finally, a group of liberal military officers rose up and attempted to force Nicholas into naming a liberal minister to resolve the issue. Nicholas now knew exactly what to do. With the aid of loyalist troops, he crushed the insurrection, hanged several of the plot's leaders, and exiled the remainder to Siberia. Ironically, it was these "Decembrists"—named after the month in which they rebelled—who put Czar Nicholas I firmly on the Russian throne.

The Decembrist uprising clearly had a profound effect on the new czar. Mistrustful of almost everyone, Nicholas favored the

A Russian cavalry camps during the Crimean War. In 1853, when Turkey refused to comply with a Russian ultimatum that Russia be given the exclusive right to protect Orthodox Christians in the Ottoman Empire, Russian troops marched into Moldavia and Walachia. Consequently, Turkey, later joined by England, France, and Sardinia, declared war on Russia and defeated the czar's forces in 1856.

liberal notions of his brother Aleksandr but had little intention of allowing them to spread. He could trust the upper class with liberal ideas—they were not a threat to the Crown—and he envisaged an enlightened hierarchy bestowing change upon a receptive people.

While Nicholas instituted cautious reform—laws were drafted that moved toward an abolition of serfdom—peasant riots continued to break out across the empire. Fed up with their dismal plight, the peasants—deeply religious, poorly educated, and indebted to the landlords—forced the more educated Russians into two groups. The Westernizers, composed of mainly young people who wished to bring democracy to Russia, admired the republics in America and France and even constitutional monarchies such as England's. They were tired of the earlier halfhearted attempts at reform. To the opposite extreme were the Slavophiles. They looked back to the days of old Russia, when the czar ruled, the landowners prospered, and the serfs worked. To them, Western ideas were dangerous and threatened the very soul of Russian life.

Czar Aleksandr II assumed the throne in a time of turmoil, when Russia was fighting its costly and losing battle with Turkey and its allies. Following the Treaty of Paris, Aleksandr II promised the Russians a new epoch of peace—a period of political, economic, and social reform. On March 3, 1861, six years after becoming emperor, Aleksandr signed the document that emancipated the serfs.

In 1848 revolution swept Europe. Infected with democracy, peoples from Italy to Austria rose up against their leaders in a bid for popular rule. What they received were bloody crackdowns. Revolution did not reach Russia, but fear and loathing did. The government immediately moved against the liberals, closing down presses, banning certain books and newspapers, and arresting radical leaders. Whatever degree of free thought had existed in Russia was quickly snuffed out.

Nicholas I died in 1855 a broken man. His reform movement was a failure; his military loss in the Crimea to Turkey, France, England, and Austria in 1854 was a lingering humiliation; and the nation was on the verge of political collapse. For the czar, the state of affairs in Russia symbolized a personal defeat, but it represented much more to Russia as a whole: Now the country had lost its middle ground, and radicals and reactionaries were squaring off for a bitter and ultimately decisive confrontation.

Aleksandr II

The reign of Aleksandr II was a turning point in Russian history because of an unstoppable tide of events and Aleksandr's willingness to go along with them. By the time Aleksandr assumed the throne in 1855, the reformist cause in Russia had grown into a revolutionary movement. The world as a whole was changing politically and economically, and autocratic Russia seemed oddly out of place. In America, for example, it was not uncommon for political opponents to accuse their adversaries of being "czarists." Aleksandr realized that Russia had to change before it was too late.

Aleksandr II faced much the same problem that had confronted so many of his royal predecessors. He needed to institute change in order to avoid revolution but could not afford to go too far for fear of creating a conservative backlash. Aleksandr began his rule by surrounding himself with liberal advisers who impressed upon him that the potentially greatest problem facing the country was serfdom. Outbreaks of rioting among the peasants were growing more frequent, and the downtrodden had found an active voice in the intelligentsia—the educated class.

The czar moved quickly. He organized the creation of numerous provincial assemblies across the empire, made up of more than 1,000 representatives of the landowners. Between 1857 and 1859 these deliberative bodies hammered out suggestions to be submitted to the central government, which was determined to overturn serfdom. Finally, on March 3, 1861, a law was approved emancipating the serfs once and for all. According to the law, each landowner had to either rent or sell a plot of his land to each of his former serfs. If the peasant chose to purchase the plot, the government would pay the landowner for the land, and the peasant would then pay back the government over a period of time. The emancipation of the serfs was undoubtedly the most sweeping reform ever undertaken by a czar; but much to Aleksandr's frustration, the freeing of the serfs seemed only to exacerbate the reigning turmoil. In 1881 the czar himself fell prey to his troubled land—Aleksandr II was assassinated by a small band of violent revolutionaries.

Nicholas II and Aleksandra Fyodorovna appear in their court robes in a 1904 photograph. Nicholas, the last czar, was unprepared to rule over the chaotic state of Russia. Massive workers' strikes, peasant uprisings, and the humiliating defeat in the Russo-Japanese War forced Nicholas to issue procedures for electing members to the first Russian parliament (Duma) in 1905.

5

Revolution and Socialism

In 1894, Nicholas II ascended the throne of Russia and, thanks in large part to his strong-willed, reactionary father, Aleksandr III, the young czar inherited a kingdom on the verge of outright revolution. The embattled landowners were struggling to preserve their way of life, radical revolutionary movements were springing up faster than the police could snuff them out, and the peasantry, though free, was seething with resentment. Freedom had not brought them prosperity.

Added to this lethal brew was Nicholas's weak character. Upon hearing the news that his father was dead, the 26-year-old prince reportedly cried to his brother-in-law: "What am I going to do? What is going to happen to me . . . to all of Russia? I am not prepared to be a czar. I never wanted to become one." Nicholas's indecisiveness plagued him from the start; he could be readily swayed by persuasive argument, and his domineering German wife, Aleksandra, could influence him at will. (She herself was under the influence of a strange, probably mad priest, Grigory Rasputin.)

But assume the throne he did, and there was much speculation that the new czar would finally bring change to Russia and avert a potential disaster. In fact, many liberals wrongly interpreted Nicholas's nonconfrontational manner as a sign of enlightenment. In another time, Nicholas II would have lived, reigned, and died a monarch who excelled more at sport than government, and so when confronted with revolutionary rumblings, he reacted instinctively. With the frightened nobility at his side, Nicholas summarily rejected any idea of a true constitutional monarchy and allowed his extensive police force, the Okhrana, to wield considerable power in attacking the numerous pockets of resistance.

He also continued the policy of "Russification" started by his father. By the beginning of the 20th century, the Russian Empire reached halfway around the globe, and the monarchy in St. Petersburg believed that it could force the numerous non-Russian peoples of the empire to effectively become "Russian." Children had to be taught in Russian, the Russian Orthodox church attempted to convert large segments of the population, and organized massacres—called pogroms—were carried out against various ethnic groups, such as the Jews.

Throughout the latter half of the 19th century, revolutionary movements began to spring up across the empire. Most were small and disorganized, and their political views tended to be poorly articulated. By the beginning of the 20th century, though, several large formal parties had been founded, and for the first time they posed a genuine threat to the Romanov dynasty. The liberals constituted the largest group. Some liberals, such as those who supported a constitutional monarchy, sat in the restored Duma, hoping to change the system from within. Others were committed to the idea of a republic. Though continually frustrated in their efforts and often exiled to Siberia, the liberals tended to have the greatest influence because they were generally reformers, not wholesale revolutionaries.

The socialists were a different matter. In 1848, a German intellectual from the middle class, Karl Marx, wrote a short but forceful book, the *Communist Manifesto*. He believed that the greed and injustice of the present system of politics would lead to worldwide revolution and the establishment of universal communism. In a Communist system the working class would rule, everything short of personal essentials would be owned by the state, and the state would determine the course of society. Marx's untried ideas were extremely attractive to many people who saw no hope in trying to reform capitalism—free markets and private ownership. These socialists, or Marxists, were of numerous minds, but all espoused the idea of total revolution.

One group in Russia, the Bolshevik (or majority) wing, was founded in 1903 under the leadership of Lenin. The Bolsheviks had splintered from their Russian socialist allies—the Menshevik (or minority) wing under Georgy Plekhanov—because Lenin and his comrades, such as Leon Trotsky, believed that a small, all-powerful leadership was needed to spark revolution and create a Communist state.

Harassed by the czar's security forces, many of the Bolsheviks, including Lenin, carried out their work in exile; some lower-level party officials, such as Joseph Stalin, instigated rebellion from within Russia itself. Their successes were few. In 1905, a popular revolt shook the monarchy—which, for a brief moment, seemed as if it would collapse—but order was violently restored. In 1906, Pyotr Stolypin became prime minister and, until his assassination in 1911, a degree of pluralism was introduced into political life. However, this pluralism at times bordered on chaos. In the end, revolution would simply have to wait.

The year 1905 also witnessed Russia's humiliating military defeat at the hands of the Japanese Empire. The year before, Japanese forces had attacked Russian positions in Manchuria and later sank much of Russia's Pacific fleet. This drove Russia into a negotiated settlement, mediated by U.S. president Theodore Roosevelt, that forced St. Petersburg to relinquish its holdings in China. Not only did Japan emerge as a world power, but the myth of Russian military prowess was completely shattered.

As Russia's situation continued to deteriorate, war suddenly broke out across Europe in 1914. Millions of not-so-eager Russians took up arms and marched off to fight the Germans and Austro-Hungarians. The Great War, now known as World War I, was the result of competing alliances and colonial disagreements. It was a struggle of epic proportions, and for the Russians in particular it was cataclysmic. Despite the lessons of Russia's humiliating defeat at the hands of the Japanese, the Russian army, large but ill equipped, fared poorly against Emperor William II's mighty German forces. By 1916 thousands of cold and starving Russian soldiers simply dropped their arms and went home. To them, it was the czar's war, not theirs.

During the bitter winter of 1916–17, Russia was at the breaking point. Women waited on long lines for food, and heating supplies were scarce. The war was going very badly, for young Russian men refused to go to the front. Meanwhile, the nobility continued to lead a life of luxury, building only further hatred against them-

The Fourth Duma meets in the woods in 1915. After increasing outbursts of persecution of such minorities as Germans, Jews, and Ukrainians, the Duma called upon Nicholas II to replace incompetent officials; to halt political, ethnic, and religious persecution; and to release all political prisoners.

Soldiers and civilians are photographed on their way to seize the Duma in Petrograd on March 11, 1917. Russia's participation in World War I, spiraling civil unrest, and rising unemployment thrust the country into a state of anarchy.

selves. Finally, on February 8, 1917, the czar's world collapsed. The February Revolution began when factory workers struck in Petrograd—its name, St. Petersburg, had been changed at the beginning of the war because it sounded too German. As factory workers poured into the streets—they were joined by students

Nicholas's army mow down a crowd of workers who pushed past barriers in Petrograd on Sunday, March 11, 1917. Nicholas, unable to restore order and having lost the capital to the revolutionaries, abdicated his throne on March 15.

and housewives—the capital suddenly bordered on anarchy. Czar Nicholas rightfully panicked and after two days of demonstrations ordered his troops to fire on the protesters; some soldiers refused the command, but others obeyed. With blood now running in the streets, Nicholas ordered the Duma to disband. The command was ignored, and the Duma formed a provisional government. Meanwhile, the Bolsheviks had come out into the open and were forming soviets, committees of local workers. On March 15, 1917, a government delegation visited Nicholas and came away with his abdication and that of his young son, Alexis. The former czar's brother, Grand Duke Michael, refused to assume the throne—after 300 years, the Russian monarchy was no more.

Civil War

For the next seven months, Russia was ruled by a formal provisional government under liberal Duma member Aleksandr Kerensky. Kerensky represented the more moderate factions in the country and, apart from the monarchists and the Bolsheviks, many Russians believed that the new regime would bring a quick

Lenin (center) and Leon Trotsky (saluting), who led the Bolsheviks in seizing power from the provisional government in October 1917, review a parade in Moscow's Red Square in 1919. Lenin, who became chairman of the Council of the People's Commissars— the first Soviet government—in November 1917, relocated his administration from Petrograd to Moscow in the spring of 1918.

end to the misery of the past two years. Instead, Kerensky vowed to pursue the war, due in large part to pressure from Russia's Western allies, who feared a German victory in the east. The economy continued to collapse, men continued to die at the front, and the people of Russia were disgusted.

The Bolsheviks, who viewed the provisional government as little more than an inevitable step toward communism, decided the time was right to act. On October 7, 1917, armed Bolshevik forces launched a coup d'état in Petrograd, forcing the disorganized and confused provisional government to flee. Kerensky himself was whisked out of the capital in the U.S. ambassador's car. The Bolsheviks were now in charge of Petrograd, though not the country itself. They did, however, sign a peace treaty with Germany, the Treaty of Brest-Litovsk, which outraged Russia's allies. The Soviets willingly relinquished much of their western territories—Finland, the Baltics, the Ukraine, and Georgia—to either the Germans or to independence movements. The treaty split even the Bolsheviks. Foreign Commissar Leon Trotsky resigned in protest, accusing the Soviet state of playing the power politics it professed to despise. Meanwhile, the anti-Bolshevik forces, known as the Whites, began to organize throughout the countryside.

The Russian civil war had begun. The Whites were an assortment of czarists, democrats, militarists, Ukrainian cossacks, and rival socialists who had little in common besides a collective hatred of the Bolsheviks. The Bolsheviks, for their part, were equally determined to hold on to the power they had seized. Few expected the Bolsheviks to survive, but under the expert hand of Leon Trotsky, one of Lenin's oldest associates and the former Bolshevik foreign commissar, the new Red Army was whipped into an effective fighting force. Soon civil conflict had spread to virtually every corner of the empire, and slowly but surely, the Bolsheviks gained the upper hand. In 1918, the Western powers sent troops to Russia in an effort to aid the Whites, though it did not help; the Bolsheviks were winning, and there was little anyone on the outside could do to prevent their victory.

Amid this carnage, the Bolsheviks moved the czar and his family to Ekaterinburg (now Sverdlovsk) in April. On July 18, 1918, Nicholas, his wife, his children, and his aides were herded into a sealed room and killed in a hail of bullets; their remains were dumped in an unmarked grave. The Bolsheviks guarding the royal family had received word from Moscow that a White force was moving toward them and that an attempt might be made to rescue the former czar. It is now believed that Lenin himself ordered the executions.

Whatever damage the civil war did not do to the country, the Bolsheviks' policies did. Lenin instituted a program called War Communism that placed the allocation of food in the hands of the government. It was a total disaster. The peasants furiously resisted the Bolsheviks who tried to take their harvests away from them; when the Bolsheviks succeeded, they shipped most of the food to the cities. As a result, Russia was gripped by one of the worst famines in history. A brief border war with Poland in 1920–21 further complicated the situation.

In 1921, a Russian family, stricken by the famine that devastated the country after the civil war, rests a while during its search for food. More than 9 million people died between 1914 and 1921: 2 million died in World War I and at least 7 million more were victims of terrorism, hunger, and disease.

Popular uprisings broke out, and in February 1921 the naval garrison at Kronstadt, just outside Petrograd, launched a failed revolt against the Bolsheviks. Lenin could see that the situation was serious, and he quickly dropped War Communism and even allowed foreign relief agencies into the country. The Bolshevik leader then crafted an economic program, called the New Economic Policy (NEP), that restored a limited free market system to Russia. Although this pleased many Russians and Westerners alike, Lenin viewed it as merely a temporary measure to be rescinded once stability was restored. Moreover, the NEP allowed for free enterprise primarily at the local level; all industry and banking remained in the hands of the state.

Victory

The capital had been moved back to Moscow, a constitution had been drawn up in 1918, and in 1922 the Union of Soviet Socialist Republics was proclaimed. The civil war was over, and most of the former Whites had either been killed or jailed, gone into exile, or joined the Bolsheviks. Lenin then set out to create the world's first Communist state.

The Bolsheviks believed that socialist revolution would soon sweep Europe, and although they were alienated from most of the world, they continued to maintain active ties to foreign revolutionary movements primarily through the Communist International (Comintern, an organization dedicated to the overthrow of capitalism). The new government did sign a treaty in 1922 with the world community's other outcast, Germany, and several Western governments, such as Great Britain, which publicly professed hatred of the Bolsheviks, permitted trade with Russia. Many of the world's intellectuals were fascinated with Soviet Russia at this time and actively promoted its ideals and goals.

On January 21, 1924, Lenin, founder of the Soviet Union, died. His death was a tremendous shock to those Russians who had supported him and to the Bolshevik leadership in particular. No one had openly considered a line of succession, and even before Lenin had been laid to rest, fierce infighting began. The Bolshevik leadership broke into two camps. On one side stood those who continued to support the NEP; with a controlled form of free enterprise, the economy had dramatically improved since the days of famine. On the other side, Leon Trotsky led a minority movement that advocated an end to the NEP and a return to complete socialism—by force, if necessary. The Trotskyists, as they came to be known, also espoused the theory of "perpetual revolution." They believed that the Soviet regime's principal objective should be the spread of worldwide revolution. Stalin, along with much of the party, rejected the idea as dangerous, opting instead to build "socialism in one country." A power struggle ensued, and in 1927 the Communist party expelled Trotsky. Shortly thereafter, he fled the country, never to return. The aging revolutionary was assassinated by a Soviet agent while living in exile in Mexico in 1940.

Joseph Stalin

In the midst of this power struggle stood Joseph Stalin. Born in 1879 in Gori, Georgia, Stalin had spent much of his adult life in czarist jails and was sent into exile in Siberia in 1913 because of his political activities. Later, he served the upper ranks of the Communist movement by becoming its general secretary. Although he lacked the intelligence and education of the party's top leaders, he made up for these shortcomings with his ability to manipulate others and his violent character. While the party's leading minds were considering the broader issues facing the new Soviet state, Stalin had quietly amassed a personal power base. He would elevate party members to positions of authority so that they, in turn, now owed allegiance to him. The general secretary would continually pit one area of the party bureaucracy against another so that no one could grow too powerful. Thus, when Lenin died, it was Stalin who controlled the inner workings of the party, and it was to Stalin that many of the country's lower-ranking officials looked for leadership.

The country was run by a collective leadership after Lenin's death. In the spring of 1928, the first Five-Year Plan was initiated. The central government set down an economic strategy, to be carried out over the next five years, whose success would largely depend on agricultural collectivization. The state would take all arable land away from the peasants; they, in turn, would be expected to work the land as "employees" of collective farms and they would be paid accordingly. Needless to say, collectivization was highly unpopular among the peasants, and resistance was fierce. The Soviets ultimately turned to force to achieve their ends.

By 1928, Stalin was emerging as the paramount leader in the Soviet Union. His power was by no means absolute, however. His greatest threat came from those within the state leadership who had been among Lenin's closest comrades, known as the "Old Bolsheviks." Trotsky was gone, but men such as Grigory Zinovyev, Lev Borisovich Kamenev, and Nikolay Bukharin had known Stalin when he was little more than a glorified clerk. Stalin realized that if he was to survive, he would have to eliminate them.

Whereas other men might have employed political maneuvering to oust their rivals, Stalin turned to wholesale murder. Beginning in 1936, a series of show trials—trials without any legal basis—were held. Day after day, former members of Lenin's inner circle were forced to listen while state prosecutors fabricated accusations of their alleged crimes against the government. Surprisingly, those who stood trial admitted to their supposed guilt. Stalin's lieutenants had used physical and psychological torture to break their victims. The lucky ones were exiled to labor camps, known as *gulags*, in Siberia; most of the Old Bolsheviks were executed.

Soon the Great Purge spread. Lower-level officials suspected of even the slightest hint of dissent disappeared, and most of the military's officer corps, from generals on down, were summarily tried and executed. And those were just the ones reported in the papers. As fear spread, it became common to turn in neighbors, friends, and family to the police; most allegations were completely false, but they did save the accuser, if only for the moment. Entire villages were wiped out for being "uncooperative." It will never be known exactly how many people died at the hands of Stalin and his henchmen—most victims were simply dumped into mass graves—but the Soviet government now admits that at least 20 million people may have perished. Western historians fear the number could be twice that.

While millions were perishing under Stalin's rule, the Soviet dictator developed a "cult of personality." He was portrayed by the regime as a great Communist, wise teacher, and friend to children. His face and words were everywhere, and many believed the propaganda.

During his reign Stalin had transformed Russia from a backward agrarian society into an industrial power. Factories produced steel, great dams harnessed the power of rivers, and airplanes and automobiles filled the Soviet Union's skies and streets. Russians enjoyed a new standard of living, and many citizens were thus willing to overlook or justify their leader's barbarity.

World War II

While Stalin continued to terrorize his own people, ominous events were unfolding in other parts of the world. In January 1933, Adolf Hitler, founder and leader of the Nationalist Socialist German Workers' (Nazi) party, had assumed the office of German chancellor. The Nazi party was an ultranationalist political move-ment bent not only upon eliminating Jews, Gypsies, and other so-called subhumans from Europe but upon world conquest as well. Hitler believed that Germany should have an empire and that it should be in the east.

Stalin soon realized that Germany was the Soviet Union's great-est threat, and he was determined to do everything possible to avert war between the two countries. His foreign policy shifted three times during the 1930s, each time coming no closer to pre-venting what Hitler secretly knew was the inevitable. The govern-ment in Moscow first tried cooperating with Germany against Britain and France, Germany's two greatest rivals. As Hitler con-tinued to increase the size of his military, Stalin attempted to create a "united front," an alliance between the Soviet Union, Britain, and France. Unfortunately for Stalin, the Western democ-racies deeply mistrusted him, in large part because of the Soviet Union's support of revolutionary movements in the West. Fi-nally, on August 23, 1939, after Hitler had marched into Austria and Czechoslovakia and the West had done nothing to stop him, Soviet officials and Nazi leaders stunned the world by signing a nonaggression pact. The world's two greatest ideological rivals were now allies.

On September 1, 1939, Germany invaded Poland, and Britain and France, which had pledged to defend Poland, subsequently declared war on Germany—World War II had begun. The pact between Germany and the Soviet Union allowed the Red Army to invade Poland from the east; Poland had won its freedom from Russia after World War I, and Stalin believed that he was only reclaiming what was rightfully his. Soon the tiny Baltic states of Estonia, Latvia, and Lithuania also succumbed to the government in Moscow, and in the winter of 1939–40, the Soviet Union attack-ed Finland, another country that had secured its freedom from Russia after the World War I. The Finns fought valiantly throughout the winter but were eventually overwhelmed by the huge Red Army.

Stalin was convinced that his cooperation with Hitler was proof that Germany had no designs on Russia; however, on the morning of June 22, 1941, 6,000 German artillery pieces heralded the start of Operation Barbarossa, Germany's invasion of the Soviet Union. Due in part to the fact that Stalin had killed most of his experienced officers during the purges, the first months of the war were difficult for the Soviets. By the fall, Hitler's forces were within 25 miles of Moscow. The Soviet government had already fled the capital, and it seemed that the regime was on the verge of annihilation. Had winter not set in to slow the German advance, the regime might have been utterly destroyed.

The year 1942 was a pivotal year in the conduct of the war. England had won the Battle of Britain and saved itself from a German invasion, but on December 7, 1941, Japan attacked the United States at Pearl Harbor, Hawaii, and, with all of the major powers at war, the Grand Alliance was formed. The Soviet Union, Britain, and the United States banded together in the fight against Germany and its Japanese and Italian partners. American war matèriel was soon pouring into both the Soviet Union and Great Britain. While the Soviets turned the tide of battle in the east, the Western allies invaded France on June 6, 1944. On May 4, 1945, Germany finally surrendered, and three months later, Japan did the same.

A series of conferences on the future of Europe was held between Stalin and his American and British counterparts, both during and after the war. The first conference, held at Yalta on the Crimea in February 1945, was perhaps the most important, for there the world was divided into spheres of influence. The agreements reached at Yalta essentially gave the Soviet Union control of Eastern Europe, its new "security zone." Germany itself would be temporarily divided between the Soviets in the east and the

British prime minister Winston Churchill (left), U.S. president Franklin Roosevelt (center), and Soviet premier Joseph Stalin (right) meet in Yalta, in the Crimea, in February 1945 to debate various issues of the war. The Big Three, as they were called, also agreed on how the map of Europe was to be redrawn after the war.

Americans, British, and French in the west. American president Franklin Roosevelt had hoped that the United States, Britain, France, and the Soviet Union would remain allies after the war, but this was not to be.

The Cold War

As peace settled across the globe in late 1945, the world faced yet another confrontation, this time between former allies. The Red Army was firmly entrenched in the nations of Eastern Europe— Poland, Hungary, Czechoslovakia, Bulgaria, Romania, and the eastern half of Germany—and Stalin had little intention of letting them out of his grip. The Soviets systematically installed Communist regimes that were responsible to no one but the government in Moscow. Democrats were either imprisoned or executed, the free press was abolished, and the borders were closed to the West. The Americans, who had emerged from the war the leaders of the Western world, moved quickly to stem the tide of Soviet expansionism. The Marshall Plan was implemented, giving billions of dollars to help Western Europe rebuild; a Western military alliance, the North Atlantic Treaty Organization (NATO), was formed in 1949; and the Federal Republic of Germany was created that same year out of the three Western occupation zones. On June

25, 1950, Communist North Korea, under Soviet sponsorship, attacked the Republic of South Korea, and the United States led forces of the recently established United Nations (UN) to war in Korea. The conflict was brought to a stalemate, from both a military and a political standpoint.

Stalin, for his part, did what he could to make certain that the West did not succeed in containing the Soviets. In 1947, he closed off Berlin to the Allies: According to previous agreement, the German capital, which was located within the Soviet occupation zone, was itself divided among the allies. The West responded by airlifting food and other supplies into their part of the city. Stalin eventually realized that he could not pressure the Americans and their allies out, and he lifted the blockade in 1948. He also created the Warsaw Pact alliance, militarily joining the Soviet Union with its puppet regimes in Eastern Europe. In 1953 the Democratic Republic of Germany (East Germany) was formed out of the Soviet zone.

In 1949, the Soviet Union detonated an atomic bomb, making it the second country (after the United States) to possess this incredibly powerful weapon. The United States could no longer threaten the Soviets with a nuclear strike, but neither could the Soviets use the weapon against the West without risking certain retribution. So began the cold war—the state of sustained, indirect confrontation between the Soviet Union and the United States and its allies. Like two scorpions in a bottle, they could not directly go to war against one another lest they bring about a nuclear disaster. Their now-indirect struggle—conducted not with arms but with power politics, economic pressure, espionage, and hostile propaganda—soon spread around the globe.

Joseph Stalin died on March 5, 1953, bringing to an end the most brutal period in all of Soviet, perhaps all of Russian, history. The true enormity of his crimes has only recently been widely recognized; for a time Stalin was actually perceived as a great leader. In

(continued on page 89)

RUSSIAN
AND
SOVIET
PAINTINGS

Overleaf: The Miracle of St. George and the Dragon *(late 15th century) is an icon (a religious image) that was painted on a wooden panel and used in devotions of the Eastern Christians. One of the tales of St. George depicts his struggle with and triumph over the dragon, a symbol of evil. In ancient Russia, St. George was considered to be the patron saint of princes, and in the mid-15th century, the image of St. George defeating the dragon became the coat of arms of Ivan III.*

In Moscow Tavern *(1916), artist Boris Kustodiev has portrayed the everyday life of coachmen warming themselves in a local tavern as they blow on saucers of hot tea. Kustodiev's son later remarked that his father said the painting "makes you think of Novgorod icons and frescos . . . red background, red faces, the same color red walls."*

Entry of the Red Army at Krasnoyarsk in 1920 *by Nikolay Nikonov depicts the welcoming of the soldiers by the exhilarated citizens of Krasnoyarsk. Founded by the cossacks in 1628 and located near gold mines in the region of Siberia, Krasnoyarsk became a center for exiles during czarist times—Lenin himself spent two months there in 1897.*

Sergey Gherasimov's Party on the Kolkhoz *(1937), which is exhibited in the State Tretyakov Gallery in Moscow, presents the camaraderie of farm workers during a meal on a collective farm. Before World War II, most people who worked on a kolkhoz were considered to be at the bottom of the social scale, and they often aspired to escape their rural life by moving to the nearest city. However, after the war, village conditions improved and houses and farms were equipped with electricity and running water. Today, in order to keep their laborers on the land, kolkhoz officials offer incentives in the form of wages and housing.*

Marc Chagall (1887–1985), who was born in Vitebsk in western Russia, painted Window in a Dacha *when he and his wife were spending their honeymoon in a small town near Vitebsk in 1915. Beyond the white curtain, the country landscape of birch trees, flowers, and foliage are transformed by Chagall into a simple, tender, and pure symbol of the power of love.*

(continued from page 80)

1942, for instance, the Soviet leader was named *Time* magazine's Man of the Year for the second time in three years: In 1939, Stalin had been allied with Adolf Hitler; in 1941, he became a U.S. ally. Today his tyranny has left him with few admirers.

Khrushchev and Brezhnev

Stalin was succeeded by Nikita Khrushchev, a longtime party official who Stalin had sent to the Ukraine to help rebuild the devastated region after World War II. Khrushchev, who became first secretary on March 15, 1953, was very different from Stalin. He was short, fat, bald, and given to alternating outbursts of humor and anger, which were falsely rumored to be induced by alcohol. Khrushchev was also a man who had grown to detest the outright barbarity of Stalin and who had denounced the former leader in a secret speech to the party in 1956. Khrushchev pursued a foreign policy that attempted to improve relations with the United States while vastly expanding Soviet contacts with the developing nations of the Third World. Beginning with the Communist takeover in China in 1949, communism began to take hold in the poorer countries, in large part because it was an ideology hostile to their former colonial masters in the West. The United States soon found itself helping pro-Western governments and movements in an effort to contain communism. A showdown between the Soviet Union and the United States over Soviet nuclear missiles in pro-Soviet Cuba in 1962 brought the world to the brink of nuclear war—the Soviet missiles were capable of hitting targets in the United States. President John F. Kennedy ordered a naval blockade to prevent the delivery of additional missiles to Cuba, and the Soviets backed down and agreed to dismantle the missile base. A year earlier, the Soviets had backed an East German plan to construct the Berlin Wall, a physical barrier dividing the old German capital, designed to prevent East Germans from fleeing to the West.

On April 12, 1961, Yury Gagarin, a 27-year-old major in the Soviet Air Force, became the first human being to travel in space. Gagarin, in the spaceship Vostok *(East), successfully completed a full orbit of the earth and is seen here six days after his epoch-making flight.*

Meanwhile, Khrushchev tried to reform the Soviet Union itself, lessening the state's hold on the economy and encouraging greater freedom of speech. This earned him wide respect from the Soviet people. He also encouraged the Soviet space program and applauded loudest when the Soviet Union launched the world's first space satellite, *Sputnik*, in 1957 and when it put the first man, Yury Gagarin, into space in 1961. But his reform policies, his "defeat" in the Cuban missile crisis, and his embarrassing public displays, such as taking off his shoe and banging it on the table at the United Nations, finally convinced potential rivals that Khrushchev had to be removed from power. The Politburo abruptly dismissed him from office in 1964, and eventually replaced him with Leonid Brezhnev.

Brezhnev was also different from his predecessors. The new Soviet chief saw his country not as a revolutionary leader but as a major world power. And the Soviet Union was, by most measures, a superpower. Under Brezhnev the Soviets expanded their con-

ventional and nuclear forces, actively supported pro-Soviet guer-
rilla movements in the Third World, and initiated what Western
commentators called the "Brezhnev Doctrine," a principle of
"limited sovereignty" whereby every Communist party is responsible not only to its own people but to all Communist countries
as well. There had been sporadic popular uprisings in Eastern
Europe since the end of World War II, the worst of which occurred
in Hungary in 1956. Soviet and Warsaw Pact forces had invaded
Hungary and restored the despised Communist regime, killing
tens of thousands of Hungarians in the process. In 1968 a similar
uprising occurred in Czechoslovakia, and in August of that year
Soviet tanks rolled in to crush the spirit of an already oppressed
people. To justify the action, Brezhnev gave the world his "doctrine," which reserved the Soviet Union's right to lend "fraternal
assistance" whenever a "friendly" government was in danger. In
other words, the Soviet Union would do anything—including
exercise military force—to keep its allies in line.

Although much of the world, particularly the United States,
saw the Soviet Union as a threat to global stability, this did not
squelch efforts on both sides to reach an understanding that
would diminish the threat of world war. In August 1970, West
German chancellor Willy Brandt concluded an agreement with
the Soviet Union that increased trade and recognized the existence of East Germany. Brandt's policy, called Ostpolitik (Eastern
Policy) earned him the respect of Western leaders and the 1971
Nobel Peace Prize. In 1972, American president Richard M. Nixon
traveled to the Soviet Union to sign the first Strategic Arms Limit-
ations Treaty (SALT I), which put numerical limits on nuclear
weapons. A short time later, General Secretary Brezhnev traveled
to Washington, D.C. In 1975, the multinational Helsinki Treaty on
European Security and Human Rights was signed, pledging each
signatory, including the Soviet Union, to respect human rights.
The era of "détente," a French diplomatic term roughly translated

as "an absence of conflict," had dawned between East and West, and to many observers it marked the beginning of the end of the cold war.

Over the next several years the United States and the Soviet Union concluded additional arms and trade agreements, but in 1979 an aging Leonid Brezhnev sent a force of more than 100,000 troops to Afghanistan, on the Soviet Union's southern border, to prop up the pro-Soviet regime. The following year, the Polish government, under Soviet pressure, outlawed Poland's pro-democracy Solidarity movement, and the threat of a Soviet invasion loomed. As the people of Afghanistan and Poland suffered under the weight of the Soviet empire, détente collapsed, and once again the cold war took center stage.

On December 1, 1989, Pope John Paul II (right) bows his head as he greets President Mikhail Gorbachev in a historic meeting in Vatican City. The heads of the Roman Catholic church and the Soviet government agreed to work to establish diplomatic ties between the two, and after the meeting Gorbachev vowed to guarantee Soviet citizens' religious freedom.

Brezhnev died in 1980, leaving behind a country wallowing in economic and political misery. The growth of the Soviet Union as a superpower had come about at the expense of the Soviet people, and for them the country's world status did little to ease a standard of living equal to many in the Third World. Brezhnev was succeeded by former KGB (State Security Committee) chief Yuri Andropov. Though a sickly old man who built a reputation as head of one of the world's most feared security agencies, Andropov was widely rumored to be a reformer. He elevated several younger men, including Mikhail Gorbachev, to the top seats of power and took tentative steps toward reform. The world would never learn precisely what kind of leader he would have been; Andropov died within two years of taking office. He was succeeded by an even older man, Konstantin Chernenko, who had been favored by Leonid Brezhnev as his successor. Chernenko was also dead within months of assuming office.

The world began to snicker at the Soviets, and the Soviet people began to cringe in embarrassment. Most of their leaders were so old that they could hardly walk on their own, much less rule effectively. But the world soon stopped laughing; for a younger leadership emerged with the professed goal of saving the superpower from itself.

Soviet soldiers holding flowers wave to a cheering crowd as 1,300 Soviet troops pull out of Kabul, Afghanistan. In May 1988, a UN-mediated agreement provided for the withdrawal of Soviet troops and the creation of a neutral state. The Soviet army completed its pullout in February 1989, and it estimated that more than 15,000 soldiers had been killed during the 9 years of civil war.

6

A New World Role

The fundamental changes that have swept the Soviet Union since the mid-1980s have had far-reaching effects. The cold war has faded, and for the first time since World War II, the Soviet Union and the West are cooperating in a number of areas, such as arms reduction, trade, and diplomatic initiatives. Soviet foreign policy is no longer overtly aggressive, and the Soviets themselves publicly downplay their superpower status.

Initial changes in the Soviet Union, both foreign and domestic, can be credited to the leadership of one man—Mikhail Gorbachev. Though his rise to power in 1985 signaled the emergence of a younger, educated reformist crop of leaders, Gorbachev singularly personified that enlightened leadership. He gave the reformers a voice and the power they would need to transform the Soviet Union from a stagnant, closed society into a modern state ready to compete in the 21st century.

President Gorbachev is the first Soviet leader since Lenin to hold a university degree and, by coincidence, a law degree as well. Gorbachev, like Lenin, is experienced in travel but, unlike Lenin, appears to have a genuine respect for the accomplishments of the West. Gorbachev is a man of considerable intellect and

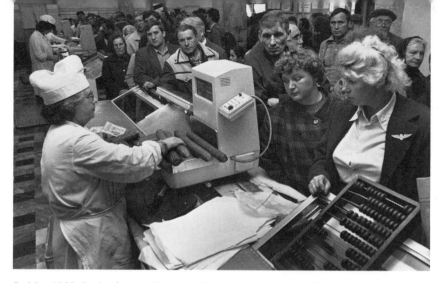

In May 1990, Soviet shoppers line up to buy sausages at a store. Major economic reforms and subsequent price rises have sparked a wave of panic buying among the Soviets.

charisma and is undoubtedly a skilled politician. He rose through the ranks of the old Soviet system, and it is questionable to what degree Gorbachev expressed his reformist views along the way.

When he assumed the position of general secretary, Gorbachev was a man little known outside the Soviet Union. He had earlier traveled to Canada and by all accounts demonstrated a willingness to work with the democracies. But no one could gauge to what extent he was prepared to alter the traditionally hostile relationship between East and West.

Gorbachev's overarching concern continues to be the state of the Soviet economy. The Soviet Union may be a military Goliath with considerable political weight, but its standard of living has never approached that of the West. Basic necessities are always in short supply, and limited quantities of essential products force people to stand in line for hours outside stores. There is a five-year waiting list to purchase an automobile. The quality of consumer goods such as clothing and household appliances is very poor.

Housing is perhaps the most serious problem. The Soviet government has never been able to meet the housing needs of the people, forcing entire families to share apartments. The housing that does exist is often substandard, lacking hot water and featuring communal bathrooms.

The reasons for this state of affairs are numerous. The state's ownership of every farm, factory, and store in the country and its insistence on directing the allocation and distribution of every raw material available have created a bureaucracy so large and inefficient that it is both corrupt and self-perpetuating. The people themselves have grown complacent, and although the state is a poor provider, it does provide. There is no incentive to work, and even if a person goes to work it has little bearing on whether or

On April 26, 1986, the Chernobyl nuclear power plant, located about 80 miles north of Kiev, exploded, spewing radioactive fragments into the air. Thirty-one people died as a result of the accident, and the long-term effects of radiation exposure on the local population and neighboring European countries will be known only in the years to come.

not his or her job will be there the next day. Money is plentiful, but there is not much to buy. Worst of all, most people are convinced that things will never improve. Consequently, the Soviet Union has the highest rate of alcoholism in the world.

President Gorbachev and his fellow reformers took a dim view of the situation, not only because a world power cannot remain one for long with such a weak economy, but because such crises breed revolt. Gorbachev believed that a series of steps had to be taken: perestroika, the decentralization of the economy and the introduction of limited free markets; glasnost, an opening of public debate through freedom of the press; and a radical reduction in the Soviet Union's military and global obligations.

The Soviet Union's military and foreign-aid expenditures are enormous. The Soviet government has revealed that expenses in these areas account for 25 percent of the Soviet Union's annual gross national product (GNP)—the total market value of all goods and services produced in a country within a given period (usually one year). The Soviet Union has maintained the largest overall military machine in the world and has had troops stationed in Eastern Europe, along the Chinese border, as well as in Asia, Africa, the Middle East, and the Caribbean for most of the past 40 years. Economic and military aid to its client states—very close allies—has been staggering. Cuba, for example, the tiny island off the coast of Florida, has until recently received approximately $5 billion every year from the Soviet Union. Vietnam, India, Nicaragua, and several African countries, including Ethiopia, Mozambique, and Angola, have also been recipients of large amounts of Soviet aid.

Being a major world power is a costly undertaking and, in the case of the Soviet Union, it is potentially bankrupting. President Gorbachev targeted the military establishment for sharp reductions, but in order to do that he has had to decrease tensions with the West. Gorbachev's approach to ending the cold war is based on the assumption that (1) the West has no intention of attacking the Soviet Union and (2) the Soviet Union and the West have enough in common that they can forge a working relationship. President Gorbachev has called this approach to world affairs New Thinking.

Under the direction of Eduard Shevardnadze, who was foreign minister from 1985 until he abruptly resigned in December 1990, the Soviet Union took numerous measures to eliminate hostility and build a sense of trust and cooperation between East and West. This was no small task. Prior to World War II, the stated aim of Soviet foreign policy had been the active overthrow of the democratic-capitalist West and the creation of a global Communist system. After the war and the collapse of the Grand Alliance, the Soviet Union's foreign policy became less ideological and more imperialistic. The Soviets systematically subjugated most of Eastern Europe to its rule, forged the Warsaw Pact, and tied those pact countries economically to the Soviet Union. As the Third World began to emerge in the 1950s and 1960s, the Soviets exploited the lingering resentments against the West in those regions by funding pro-Communist rebel groups and actively undermining the governments in power. Meanwhile, the Soviet military expanded at a staggering rate, and its nuclear arsenal eventually equaled the nuclear arsenals of the United States, Britain, and France.

For most of the 20th century, the West committed itself to preventing the further spread of the Soviet empire. The United States in particular tailored its military and foreign policy to check Soviet ambitions. Occasionally, overtures toward a more cordial relationship were made, first in the late 1950s and again in the early 1970s, but neither side was willing to trust the other. Thus, when Gorbachev began to open the lines of communication with the Soviet Union's old adversaries, most in the West questioned his sincerity, and many Soviets doubted his wisdom.

Thousands of Lithuanians demonstrate in the streets of the capital city of Vilnius in August 1989. "Nationalist hysteria" in the Baltic republics is a continuing concern of the Kremlin, which is struggling to control those citizens who resent Soviet rule.

Two principal factors greatly contributed to the new Soviet foreign policy. First, Ronald Reagan had been elected president of the United States in 1980, in part, by taking a tough, outspoken stance against the Soviet Union. He referred to the Soviet Union as an "evil empire," embarked upon the largest peacetime military buildup in American history, and implored Gorbachev to tear down the Berlin Wall. President Gorbachev realized that any attempt by his country to match the United States militarily might well bankrupt the already suffering Soviet economy.

Second, and perhaps more significant, popular revolt spread like wildfire throughout Eastern Europe in late 1989. The people of Eastern Europe had always harbored a deep hatred of the Communist system imposed on them after the World War II. They were aware of how their European brothers lived in the West and resented being subjected to Soviet domination. They had risen up several times before, in 1953, 1956, 1968, and again in 1970, and each time were brutally suppressed. In each instance revolt had been limited to one country; in 1989, however, East Europeans took to the streets from one end of the region to the other. The Poles had started the process by exacting significant concessions from their government, proving that the eastern European regimes were not invincible. Faced with the prospect of regional chaos, President Gorbachev broke precedence by permitting—and at times quietly encouraging—these popular movements. By the end of 1989, the Communist regimes of Poland, East Germany, Hungary, Czechoslovakia, Bulgaria, and Romania had fallen, often peacefully, sometimes violently. Democracy had come to Eastern Europe, due largely to Gorbachev's willingness to relinquish the Soviet Union's western empire.

There was now no doubt as to Gorbachev's sincerity. And the Soviet leader continued to make radical changes in his country's world role. He informed many of the Soviet Union's longtime allies, such as Cuba, that his country would no longer be a source of unlimited aid. He joined the West in hammering out diplomatic solutions to many regional disputes—such as those in Angola, Cambodia, and Central America—and rejected many Third World nations' appeals to anti-Western sentiment. In November 1989, Gorbachev did nothing to prevent East and West Germans from toppling the Berlin Wall, and he acceded to popular German and Western demands that the two Germanys finally be reunited, going so far as to agree to a greater Germany's membership in NATO.

China

The Soviet Union's tense relations with the United States and the West are well known and documented, but interestingly, it is its giant Communist neighbor to the south that is one of the Soviet Union's most unyielding enemies. When the Chinese Communist party, under the leadership of Mao Zedong, came to power in 1949, the Soviet Union acquired its first real ideological ally. Unlike the regimes of Eastern Europe and Mongolia (which fell under Soviet-dominated Communist rule in 1924), the Communist government of China had strong popular roots and voluntarily allied itself with the government in Moscow. Throughout much of the 1950s, the Soviets and Chinese Communists closely cooperated in a number of areas—the Soviets were instrumental in helping China industrialize—but China's leadership refused to bow to the Soviets, and in 1959 strains in the relationship began to show.

The Chinese were committed to a confrontational approach toward the West, largely because of the United States's defense of Formosa (now Taiwan)—the island to which the anti-Communist Nationalists had fled after the long Chinese civil war. The Chinese openly criticized the Soviets for their more cordial relations with the West, and Premier Khrushchev openly criticized the Chinese in return. Soon the war of words escalated, and the Chinese accused the Soviets of splitting the international Communist movement along racial lines. Herein lay the real issue.

Much of the Russian psyche has been shaped by the long and violent Tatar occupation; in a sense, the Chinese were the Tatars' descendants. (In fact, the Mongolians were descended from the Tatars.) To an outside observer such a conclusion seems somewhat unjustified, but ethnic animosities do not abate easily. Furthermore, the Soviets had sided with the Chinese Nationalists during the 1920s, a fact not quickly forgotten by the Chinese Communists. Twentieth-century ideological differences only aggravated these lingering tensions; by the end of the 1960s, both sides of the Sino-Soviet border bristled with armies, and skirmishes became common. For the next two decades the Soviets and Chinese remained entrenched adversaries. Diplomatic relations were not broken, but there were no high-level meetings, and trade between the two countries was kept at a minimum.

President Gorbachev's efforts to lessen tensions around the world were not limited to the West, and, on May 20, 1989, he became the first Soviet leader to visit China in 30 years. There was general agreement that ties should be improved, but at the time, China's leaders were less interested in relations with the Soviet Union than in ties with their own people. Gorbachev had arrived at a moment of tremendous social unrest in China. Beijing and China's other major cities, such as Shanghai, were in the grip of massive student-led prodemocracy demonstrations that threatened Communist rule.

Trade

It cannot be overstated that much of Gorbachev's impetus in foreign affairs comes from a desire to salvage the Soviet economy. His reasons for making so many concessions to the West are more than simply humanitarian—the Soviet Union desperately needs expanded Western trade. The West has been reluctant to trade with the Soviet Union for two reasons: First, there has been a concerted effort to keep high technology out of the hands of the Soviet military. Computer technology, in particular, is critical to a modern army, and it is well-known that Soviet computers are generations behind those of the West.

Second, Soviet currency, the *ruble*, is nonconvertible; that is, it cannot be traded for Western currencies because it is not based on a universal standard, such as gold or silver. In essence, Soviet money is worthless in the non-Communist world. This has meant that the Soviets must acquire Western goods with either hard currency, such as gold, or by swapping something that the West needs. Both systems are flawed and neither lends itself to extensive commerce. The Soviet Union, along with South Africa, is one of the world's leading producers of gold, but the Soviets have a limited supply and cannot afford to entirely deplete their reserves. Trading goods can work, but only if each side consistently has something that the other side wants. With the exception of items such as caviar and vodka, Soviet consumer goods are greatly inferior to those of the West and free Asia. The Soviet Union does have extensive natural resources—it is the world's leading producer of oil and natural gas—but most raw materials are difficult to exploit because of both the country's severe climate and geography and its out-of-date technology. Gorbachev and his economic advisers are considering the idea of making the ruble convertible but are stymied by what effect it might have on the economy. Nevertheless, expanded trade is still highly desirable. The Soviets, for example, have offered to provide the United States with oil if the United States will provide the technology to remove it from the ground.

Gorbachev would also like to see a massive infusion of Western investment. From the Soviet standpoint, the most desirable arrangements are joint ventures, whereby a Western company

On February 25, 1990, about 100,000 protesters converge on Moscow's Zubovsky Square in one of the largest prodemocracy rallies ever held in the Soviet capital. By the end of 1989, the Communist regimes of many Eastern European countries had fallen, the Berlin Wall had been toppled, and prodemocracy demonstrations within the Soviet Union escalated.

enters into partnership with a Soviet enterprise to create a larger business. The Western partner brings capital, technology, and know-how to the Soviet Union and receives, in return, a sizable percentage of the profits. In a land of almost 285 million people, the potential for new markets is theoretically limitless. Several such ventures have already been tried, but two recurring problems are hampering the process. First, because the ruble is non-convertible, Westerners are forced to keep their profits inside the Soviet Union, taking them home in the form of goods. Many therefore demand their profits in Western currency. This denies the joint enterprise access to the Soviet market—where potential consumers have only rubles—and does nothing for the Soviet consumer. Some Western corporations, such as McDonald's, the American fast-food chain, are willing to accept the ruble as payment, but this is a rarity.

What is most important is that the Soviets have opted to replace confrontation with peaceful trade. Over the course of 70 years, the Soviet Union has transformed itself from exporter of revolution to imperial aggressor to cooperative world partner. Perhaps this is proof that the Bolsheviks' dream of a worldwide Communist state was little more than that, a dream; it is a hard lesson that aggression ultimately leads nowhere.

In April 1988, about 50 Kurds demonstrate near Moscow's Red Square to protest the alleged use of chemical weapons by Iraq against the Kurdish town of Halabjah. Many of Iraq's high-ranking military officers have received training in the Soviet Union.

7

Government and Society

The Communist party of the Soviet Union is the bedrock of the Soviet state; it founded the regime and gives the government its legitimacy. Lenin and the first Bolsheviks defined the party as the source of all authority and the arbiter of all power. The state was to be its practical extension, and the party's ideals were to be the only source of guidance. The first Soviet constitution bestowed sole political power on the Communist party, and for almost 70 years the party was above question in all matters great and small.

Officially, the government and the party are not one and the same, though each is clearly intended to serve the interests of the other. In fact, virtually everyone who serves in the government is a party member, making the party organization the true seat of power in the Soviet Union. Lenin defined the party as a ruling elite, and that is how it has remained. A party congress is convened every four years to elect the Central Committee, which then elects a ruling council, called the Politburo, and the organizational Secretariat. Traditionally, the Politburo has approximately 20 members, of whom only half are eligible to vote in council; the nonvoting members are referred to as candidates. The true power within this closed echelon rests with the secretary-general of the Secretariat. Also a Politburo member, he is the supreme leader of the Communist party and, by extension, is usually the leader of the Soviet Union as well.

Membership in the Soviet Communist party has always been severely limited—only six percent of the population belongs—and party members have traditionally been the most privileged people in society. Communist indoctrination begins at an early age, and schoolchildren are encouraged to join Komsomol, the party's youth league. Those who excel are taken under the party's wing to be groomed as future leaders. They are sent to the best universities and, if all goes according to plan, are allowed membership in the party. Social and career advancement is normally impossible without party membership. The best jobs are given to members, and the best apartments are reserved for their use. Private vacation homes, or dachas, located in the countryside or at the seashore, are given to those who rise to the top of their profession, whether in government, science, or sports. The party's financial holdings are enormous; it owns resorts and spas around the country for use by its top officials. In a land where most people live at subsistence levels, those in the party are often granted access to Western consumer goods and enjoy free trips abroad.

Delegates attend a Communist party conference in Moscow on June 19, 1990. Party leaders are elected by the Central Committee, which is in turn chosen by regional party organizations.

The Old System

The first Soviet constitution, adopted on July 6, 1923, vested the central government with enormous power. The Congress of Soviets was the supreme ruling body and regularly met once every two years. Daily state operations were the responsibility of the Central Executive Committee, formed from the Soviet of the Union and the Soviet of Nationalities. The Central Executive Committee itself was governed by the Presidium, and it was here that power resided. Because the Soviets were aware of potential national unrest, the first constitution permitted the 15 republics the right to peacefully secede from the union. The first government of the Soviet Union was highly complex, but it was the only way that the Communists could centralize their control without denying nominal representation at the local level.

The All-Union Congress of Soviets adopted a new constitution on December 5, 1936, which theoretically expanded democratic representation. The All-Union Congress was replaced by the two-chambered Supreme Soviet. Its members were elected every four years, and when not in session, its Presidium would conduct its daily business. The Council of Ministers was also established. Consisting of experts rather than politicians, its role was to oversee the organs of government.

The government system at the regional and local levels was, and remains, a labyrinth of committees, assemblies, and unions. The central constitution called for each republic to have its own system of government, each of which closely paralleled the central structure, and each of which was given a degree of authority over its affairs. Through the Kremlin's pervasive power, though, genuine autonomy was limited, and no action could be taken in any republic without the consent of the Kremlin. The Soviet structure of government also reached down to the workplace and the city block. The soviets, the local political organizations, were the foundation on which the state rested; for it was from these that the first state emerged after the revolution, and its was through the soviets that the Kremlin could control daily life.

After 1936 other changes were made and other constitutions were drafted, as in 1977; still, the often confusing structure that was the Soviet government remained fundamentally unaltered. The Soviets have always had the problem of maintaining absolute control while being nominally democratic; the very complexity of the system is an extension of that dilemma.

A Closed Society

The state touches almost every aspect of every citizen's life, whether or not he or she is a Communist party member. Each child's abilities, for example, are gauged at an early age, and the state subsequently determines in what areas that individual will excel. Exhibiting a particular skill as a student may well set the course of one's entire work life. The party, the state, and society were intended to be one and the same.

In entertainment and the arts, the state has traditionally dictated what people can and cannot view. During the 1920s and 1930s, the notion of "socialist morality" became a label for social control. The early Communists believed that permissiveness was a direct result of capitalist "decadence" and that it was the state's responsibility to establish a code of social conduct. This became especially true during the post–World War II era, when rock music emerged as an integral part of Western culture. From music to clothing, the Soviets officially sanctioned or banned whatever they liked or disliked. However, over the past 10 years or so, the Soviets have deferred to the will of the people. It is not uncommon to see Western musicians, such as Paul McCartney and Billy Joel, playing to thousands of Soviet fans. Also, American jazz has always been especially attractive in the Soviet Union.

In art as well, the Soviets have historically determined norms of acceptability. While they were developing a code of "socialist morality," the Soviets also developed their own approach to art, known as "socialist realism." The Bolsheviks came to power at a time when modernism was finally being recognized as a distinct art form; for the Bolsheviks, however, it failed to illustrate to the masses the state's ideal "Soviet man." Soviet art—that which is officially sanctioned by the state—was close in style to the realism of the 18th and 19th centuries. The works of such artists as Arkady Plastov depicted Soviet life in all its glory—or imagined glory— complete with heroic Soviet figures bravely defending socialism and happy collective farmers content in their work. This trend carried over into literature, as dramas and novels played on class themes.

Film especially became a vehicle for the state's message. Very early movies, such as the silent film *The Battleship Potemkin*, which glorified a naval mutiny during the reign of Nicholas II, set a precedent. For years after World War II, the Soviet film industry seemed almost incapable of producing anything but melodramatic recants of Soviet victories against the Germans. To most, Soviet "realism" was little more than Soviet propaganda.

Terror

The Soviet state has existed as a dictatorship for most of its 70 years and during that time has perfected the means for controlling virtually every aspect of society. It is due to this that Soviet-style dictatorship has lasted as long as it has. It is easy enough to control what is written and what is reported, to determine where people can go and what they can do, but it is another matter to harness society itself and transform it into the vehicle of an ideology. However else Lenin's vision of a Communist state may have failed, his plan for an entire society affected by a single political view was, for a time, a wide success.

Lenin's plan has not been a total success, though, because the state could never blindly trust the people to follow its lead. Consequently, the element of terror was introduced into society. One of the first measures of power Lenin took when he assumed leadership was to create a security organization—the Cheka—under the leadership of Polish-born Felix Dzerzhinsky. Later known under Stalin as the NKVD and now recognized as the KGB (Komitet Gosudarstvennoi Bezopasnosti), this internal police agency enforced the rule of the party at home, destabilized governments abroad, and spied on foreign adversaries. Within the Soviet Union itself, the KGB became an empire within an empire and, through a network of paid professionals and reliable informers, was capable of squelching dissent in its earliest stages. At the height of its power, the KGB was responsible to but a few selected leaders in Moscow—and, reportedly, at times not even to them. The power of the KGB had always been extensive, and under the influence of a tyrant like Joseph Stalin, it was almost unlimited, its cruelty rarely paralleled. It is surprising, therefore, that the KGB emerged as one of the original proponents of change in the Soviet Union.

In 1986, a Moldavian student reports his developments on an invention to improve electric engines and pumps. Many Soviet students are members of scientific societies that work to make factories and utilities more efficient and economical.

Education, Law, and Social Services

Despite the repressive nature of the Soviet regime, compared to life under the czars, the average citizen does benefit from public services. Health care and education are free, food and housing costs are stabilized, and legal representation is state provided. The quality of these services, however, belies their effectiveness.

Soviet health care on a mass scale is notoriously poor; the country suffers from chronic food shortages; housing, if it can be found, is substandard; the legal system has traditionally been an instrument of state terror; and the educational system, though generally quite good, frequently denies individual choice at higher levels. Whatever the relative shortcomings, though, the Soviet people welcome the regime's giving hand. The Soviets have made life less anxious, if no less oppressive, than it had been under the monarchy.

Women

The role of women has changed significantly under the Communists. Women in czarist Russia maintained a status similar to their Western peers. Women from across the social range played the traditional role of wife, mother, and homemaker. Those from the middle and upper classes were educated but were rarely permitted to pursue careers or attain positions of importance. Today Soviet women work, are educated, and are given the same rights as men. They are cosmonauts—the Soviet Union put the first woman into space—scientists, educators, and politicians. President Gorbachev's wife, Raisa, for example, holds a doctorate and has taught at the university level.

However, as in most societies, Soviet attitudes toward women generally remain unchanged. Traditionally, at least one woman sits on the Politburo, though a woman has yet to attain a true policy-making position in the government. Soviet women frequently complain that their men refuse to help them in the home.

Although there have been marked improvements in the situation of Soviet women, there is still room for advancement.

Sports

Its athletic program is a source of pride and joy for the Soviet Union. For the past three decades, Soviet athletes have been a dominant force in international competition. The Soviet Union has excelled in such areas as hockey, track and field, gymnastics, swimming, weight lifting, and now even tennis. The Soviets regularly rank near the top at the Olympic Games and in other competitions, including the Goodwill Games. Competitors such as Olga Korbut, one of the greatest gymnasts of all time, have elevated Soviet athletes to among the finest in the world.

The Soviets' sports programs have long come under criticism from much of the international community, however. Amateur athletics practically does not exist in the Soviet Union. As with most of their accomplishments, the Soviets expend considerable resources to develop their athletics. The best sportsmen are weed-

The Soviet gymnast Olga Korbut performs her routine on the balancing beam at the 1972 Olympic Games in Munich. Korbut, whose vitality and mastery inspired athletes around the world, won three gold medals at the 1972 Olympics.

In October 1990, Anatoly Karpov (left) and Gary Kasparov compete in the World Chess Championship, which opened in New York City. Chess is a very popular game in the Soviet Union.

ed out at an early age and brought to elaborate training facilities. By the time an athlete reaches international competition, sports has become his or her career. Those who achieve greatness are rewarded with homes, cars, and national accolades.

Most international competition, though, is strictly amateur. Western athletes, for example, are forbidden to receive payment for competing and are barred from national teams if they do. It is understandable, then, that the Soviet Union's sponsorship of its athletes raises certain questions. The use of drugs, such as steroids, is also forbidden. Traditionally, the Soviets have refused to allow their athletes to be tested for drug use. Critics argue that if Soviet athletes do not use steroids, then there should be no objection to testing.

Government Today

Beginning in 1989, the younger leaders of the Soviet Union acknowledged that the existing bureaucratic government was oppressive, unresponsive to the will of the people, and corrupt. They believed that the country had to be changed in several areas, beginning with the government itself.

Under the present system, adopted in early 1990, the central government is headed by a president who is elected by the national legislature. The president, invested with sweeping powers, appoints a prime minister who is officially responsible for the government's operation and who remains, in fact, subordinate to the will of the president.

The president rules with the assistance of an executive advisory committee, similar to the American president's cabinet. Here the president assembles those he considers to be the country's most competent authorities in areas ranging from economic planning to drafting of legislation. The members have varied backgrounds— some serve in government, others come from academia, and there are even those who have made their name as writers. The president can also turn to the Politburo for advice. With the changes of 1990, the once all powerful Politburo was expanded to include regional leaders but was simultaneously stripped of much of its authority.

There has been no greater development in recent years than the creation of a democratically elected Supreme Soviet in 1989. For the first time in Soviet history, citizens were given the opportunity to elect genuine representatives. Before then, "elected" officials were handpicked by the Communist party and usually ran unopposed. The elections of 1989, then, were unlike any the country had ever seen. Orthodox Communists openly battled with former dissidents, and former security officers jousted with moderate economic reformers. The new legislature represents a significant cross section of the Soviet Union and has become the scene of many heated battles over the future of the country. Laws and programs can only take effect if they are approved by the Supreme Soviet, and its members use their newfound authority with zeal.

The president himself, who presides over this deliberative body, can often be seen throwing his hands up in exasperation while the hall rocks with the sound of free debate.

The political changes taking place at the top have developed hand in hand with the fundamental changes taking place in society itself. President Gorbachev came to power believing that a more open society—a society in which every citizen may speak his or her mind without fear of persecution—would be the driving force behind a revitalized economy. Today there is unprecedented freedom of expression in the Soviet Union. Newspapers and magazines have sprung up that regularly assail the government and its leaders on a variety of counts. The official publications of the government, the party, and the military, such as *Pravda* and *Izvestia*, no longer take direction from those they were created to serve. Television now features investigative-reporting shows that expose the worst side of Soviet life. Government officials now face tough questioning from Soviet broadcasters. Books long banned as "counterrevolutionary," such as Boris Pasternak's *Doctor Zhivago* (1957) and Aleksandr Solzhenitsyn's *Gulag Archipelago* (1973), are being published, and foreign works are being made available to eager Soviet readers. Soviet society is alive as never before, and it is unlikely that the Soviet people will ever relinquish their newfound voice.

In Kishinev, Moldavia, demonstrators carry a portrait of Gorbachev along with Romanian and Moldavian flags, in open defiance of a Central Committee statement made in August 1989 condemning the rise of nationalist unrest in the Soviet Union. In January 1991, Soviet troops used force to quell the independence movement in the Baltics; the Kremlin's crackdown on the democracy movement was expected to spread to other republics as well.

8

An Uncertain Future

The Soviet Union is headed down a road from which there is no turning back, mainly because the Soviet people are enjoying unprecedented levels of freedom to their fullest advantage. They have been at liberty to elect true representatives; to hold their leaders accountable for their deeds; to question both the state and its ideology; to publish and read what they wish; and to express their opinions without fear. The government has systematically stripped itself of much of its power, admitted its past mistakes, and made peace with the world. The Soviet Union is undergoing nothing less than a revolution, complete with all the hopes and fears that are part of every great upheaval.

Life under both the czars and the Communists has never been easy; economic and physical suffering without the freedom to stand up for one's inalienable rights has had a profound impact on the people of this vast land. The outside world, in fact, assumed that the Soviet people, if not content in their plight, had somehow resigned themselves to a life of quiet misery. All that has changed. The people have put their leaders and the world on notice that they are neither content nor willing to accept a future similar to the past. The world can do little more than watch with amazement and wait to see how this grand drama will end.

This transformation, as encouraging as it may be, is fraught with danger. Gorbachev's early reform measures were accepted by the peoples of the Soviet Union with wariness, but once convinced of their new leader's desire to fundamentally alter society, the Soviet people took the lead in building a new Soviet Union. And now the country teeters on the brink of chaos.

Two main factors are contributing to the breakdown of Soviet society and government. First, Gorbachev's policy of perestroika—the restructuring of the economy—has actually led to worsening economic conditions. The reformers were intent on introducing a free market system in which private citizens own the factories, stores, and farms and production is determined by demand. The transition from a state-controlled economy has been difficult simply because it has never been tried on such a large scale. As a result, there have been wide shortages of such basic necessities as bread, potatoes, and fuel. Furthermore, the government has moved to close unprofitable state enterprises, thus cre-

In October 1990, Soviet soldiers harvest potatoes near Moscow. Although the Soviet Union grows enough food to feed itself, the distribution system is collapsing—food often sits rotting in fields and warehouses.

In July 1989, striking coal miners in Siberia read a newspaper during a rally. Despite Gorbachev's warnings that strikes would endanger his economic reforms, labor unrest continued to spread.

ating a rise in unemployment. Homelessness is widespread. The people have understandably grown angry and afraid and are holding their leaders directly responsible for the deteriorating situation. Workers, such as those of Siberia's coal mines, openly demand a better standard of living and have used massive strikes to pressure the government. It is not uncommon to see tens of thousands of protesters marching outside the Kremlin, calling for the resignation of the government.

Second, the Communist party has fallen into complete disrepute. As the mechanism that has held the country together for the last 70 years, the Communist party now appears impotent, and the people openly blame it, its socialist policies, and its wide corruption for ruining the country. Despite whatever ills the party may have brought on society, nothing has emerged to take its place, and with its demise has come a breakdown of central rule. One republic after the next has declared a degree of independence from the party and the government, often with dire consequences.

Popular movements have sprung up across the country, and none are more potent than those in the Russian Federation. With the new openness has come a revival of Russian culture. Glasnost has, on one hand, been a vehicle for a religious rebirth. The long-persecuted Russian Orthodox church is restoring its places of worship, and young people are turning toward their nation's spiritual center. There have even been calls for a restoration of the monarchy, and many Leningraders wish to give their city back its original name, St. Petersburg. On the other hand, organizations such as Pamyat, which means "Memory," are calling for a "cleansing" of Russian life. Like the Slavophiles of the 19th century, they reject links with the West, and they blame Jews for bringing communism to Russia.

The overwhelming majority of Russians do not support these extremist movements, but many do support political leaders who openly reject the Communist party and those who rule in its name. Perhaps the most important of this new breed of populist is Boris Yeltsin. Yeltsin earned national prominence as a loyal Communist who served as member of the Politburo in the mid-1980s. He soon broke with Gorbachev, the very man who put him in that position, and was eventually ousted from the top leadership in 1987. Yeltsin recognized the popular outrage against the govern-

Boris Yeltsin (center), a former ally of Gorbachev and former member of the Politburo, campaigns for the presidency of the Russian Federation in May 1990. Yeltsin, who won the election, has openly criticized Gorbachev for not moving quickly enough to establish a free market economy. On February 19, 1991, after observing the accumulation of "absolute personal power" by Gorbachev and the country's growing economic despair, Yeltsin called for Gorbachev's resignation on national television.

ment and used his political abilities to align himself with the people. He won a seat in the new Supreme Soviet and eventually the presidency of the Russian Republic. Seen at first as little more than an opportunist, Yeltsin has earned genuine respect at home and abroad. He advocates a complete end to the rule of the Communist party and to the rigid economic and political control it wields over society. As the Russian Federation's leader, Yeltsin has instituted his own radical reforms for the republic. Even President Gorbachev, who is reported to privately loathe the outspoken Yeltsin, has joined with him in carrying out a series of measures designed to create a market economy for the entire country. Boris Yeltsin is so popular among Soviets from across the anti-Communist political spectrum that he is favored as a successor to Gorbachev.

A Return to the Past

By the dawn of 1990, Soviet society had split into two warring camps, the reformers and the reactionaries, neither of whom were content with the country's apparent downward slide. President Gorbachev, once the radical of Soviet society, gradually found himself on the defensive, accused both of not moving far enough fast enough and of leading the country toward total collapse. Gorbachev's political skills had traditionally served him well, allowing him to keep his feet in both camps while steering a middle course. But increased ethnic tensions, a disintegrating economy, civil disorder, and anxious party and military leaders finally forced Gorbachev into taking sides.

Reformers could clearly sense Gorbachev's wavering commitment to change, but it was not until December 20, 1990, that their fears were confirmed. In an impassioned speech before the Soviet parliament, Foreign Minister Eduard Shevardnadze, an architect of Gorbachev's New Thinking, abruptly resigned his post to "protest against the advance of dictatorship," though he could not, or would not, say from where it would come. President Gorbachev, who had asked the Supreme Soviet for expanded powers to help him deal with the spiraling economic and civil strife, was shocked by his longtime ally's speech and insulted by its insinuation. He immediately replied that for Shevardnadze to quit during "this difficult moment is unforgivable." (Gorbachev replaced Shevardnadze with Aleksandr A. Bessmertnykh, an English-speaking career diplomat.)

Shevardnadze's message became clearer when, during the last week of December, the Congress of People's Deputies voted to give Gorbachev absolute control over the executive branch of government and authority to rule by decree if necessary. In addition, the Congress confirmed Gorbachev's choice for the first vice-president of the Soviet Union, Gennady Yanayev, a conservative party bureaucrat. Many understood these developments to be the dictatorship of which Shevardnadze had spoken.

Gorbachev's former domestic allies continued to watch as conditions deteriorated by the day. On January 13, 1991, Soviet tanks plowed into a crowd of hundreds of unarmed nationalists in Lithuania's capital city of Vilnius. Fifteen people were killed and more than 100 were wounded. After the attack, the National Salvation Committee, a shadowy pro-Kremlin group wishing to overthrow the elected, independence-minded Lithuanian government, seized the broadcast facilities and television studios in Vilnius and claimed to have taken over the city. The Soviet army's sudden show of force was the largest there since Lithuania had declared independence nearly one year earlier. Lithuanians and their Latvian neighbors, who were themselves attacked shortly thereafter, quickly formed civilian militias, declaring that they would rather die than capitulate to the Kremlin.

Emboldened Soviet newspapers immediately lashed out at Gorbachev, blaming him for the army's violence in the Baltics. Gorbachev responded by calling for the suspension of press freedoms. At first unwilling to answer the question of who had given the order to open fire on civilians, Gorbachev later claimed that it was not the Kremlin but local military commanders who had taken action. He went on to blame the Baltics' separatist leadership itself for bringing on the bloodshed by leaving the military no choice but to apply force. He then renewed his call for press censorship during such crises.

Gorbachev's strong-arm tactics accelerated as the month wore on. In an effort to crush the thriving black market, Moscow suddenly announced that citizens had only 3 days to exchange their 50- and 100-ruble notes for smaller bills. Large ruble bills are a mainstay of the black market. (Gorbachev's personal economic adviser, Nikolai Y. Petrakov, resigned in mid-January 1991 over the president's retreat from a free market system.) At the same time, the Kremlin announced that the army would patrol the streets of major cities jointly with local police forces in an effort to control a growing crime wave. Days later, President Gorbachev invested the KGB with extensive powers of search and seizure.

Soviet reformers, and much of the world, have been perplexed by Gorbachev's slide toward dictatorial rule. There are any number of explanations for his actions. Many observers believe that hard-liners from the military, the KGB, and the party gave Gorbachev an ultimatum: Either restore order or step down. If this was the case, then Gorbachev had lost his political free will. However, it is often forgotten that Gorbachev's original calls for perestroika and glasnost were designed to improve the existing order, not to overthrow it. Gorbachev himself, therefore, may have grown intolerant enough of the resulting chaos that he instinctively moved to crack down on dissent. Finally, for all of Gorbachev's displeasure with the present system, he is, by his own admission, a committed Leninist. Lenin argued that it was often necessary on the road to progress to take one step backward for every two forward. Perhaps Gorbachev believed that the time had come to take a step backward, to consolidate recent advancements while eliminating potentially devastating side effects.

Whatever motivated Gorbachev to turn on his earlier principles, his actions only further reflect the dilemma that has repeatedly plagued so many of the nation's rulers. Russia has always been a land crying out for reform, for enlightened leadership, yet successive reform movements have inadvertently succeeded in opening a Pandora's Box. Reactionary versus reformer, Slavophile versus Westernizer, Communist versus democrat, Russia—the Soviet Union—is a society forever at war with itself and almost every reform leader has eventually had to apply force in order to avert catastrophe. Indeed, it is said that many Russians would prefer a strong hand at the top rather than none at all.

One of the most gnawing questions for the West is, what, if anything, should it do about the Soviet Union? The Soviet Union is still a very powerful country, with an enormous military, and it wields considerable political influence around the world. (In 1990, the United States and its allies could never have received a United Nation's mandate to liberate Iraqi-occupied Kuwait without the Soviet Union's cooperation.)

When Gorbachev rose to power in 1985 and quickly began his program of reform, he was accepted as a hero in the West. He was nothing like his predecessors; he was young, educated, charismatic, and he made every effort to build a new relationship with his country's old enemies. Once Gorbachev earned the trust of Westerners, he took on almost mythical proportions, and, increasingly, Western policymakers placed much of their hopes for a new, less aggressive Soviet Union on this one man. Critics warned that, should Gorbachev fall from power or permanently change direction in his policies, the West's new relationship with Moscow might well fall by the wayside.

There is very little the West can do to affect the course of Soviet internal events. The political unrest in the Soviet Union is a uniquely Soviet problem and can be resolved only by the Soviet people themselves. But the West has done much in the way of trade to shore up the Soviet Union's deteriorating internal situation and give a boost to the reform movement, for prolonged economic chaos will surely lead to popular revolt, which, in turn, could lead to a reactionary takeover. Such a regime would certainly take a more hostile stance toward the West. Many continue to believe that infusions of capital from Western Europe, the United States, and Asia, either in the form of joint ventures or trades of consumer goods for raw materials, can affect the deepening Soviet crisis to some degree.

There are those in the West, however, who have argued from the beginning that outside assistance will only serve to prop up a dying Communist system, the system against which the West struggled for so long. Clearly, in the wake of Gorbachev's authoritarian shift, they were right: Aid did not necessarily lead to a peaceful transition to a non-Communist system in the Soviet Union. (In fact, Western nations that had earlier pledged billions of dollars in aid to the Soviet Union moved to suspend that aid following the crackdown in the Baltics.) In the long run, there are no answers. And it is best to remember that Americans are only passive observers to events of historic proportion.

American writer John Reed referred to the beginning of the 1917 Bolshevik Revolution as "ten days that shook the world." Indeed they were. A revolutionary movement bent upon destroying the old world order had seized control of one of the world's largest and most powerful empires. And for the next 70 years, many of the world's nations largely defined themselves against this phenomenon called the Soviet Union. Today the world again watches as that vast power to the east wrestles with itself. And again the world shakes.

GLOSSARY

balalaika   A traditional six-stringed triangular instrument resembling a guitar.

Bolsheviks   Translated as "majority," it is the name given to those Communists led by Lenin who broke with their fellow revolutionaries in 1903. They are later referred to as the Soviets.

boyars   The landowners who ruled at the regional and local levels during the reign of the czars.

dacha   A vacation home usually located in the mountains or near the water. Dachas are given to the very top government leaders and to those individuals who excel in their profession.

détente   A French diplomatic term loosely translated as "absence of hostility." It most commonly refers to the period of cooperation between the United States and the Soviet Union during the 1970s.

Duma   The council of the boyars that officially shared power with the czars and local land councils.

glasnost   Translated as "openness," it is the name Gorbachev has given to his program of encouraging free speech and popular debate.

Komsomol   The Communist party's youth organization.

krmyl   Translated as "outpost," it was usually a fortified trading post.

perestroika   Translated as "restructuring," it is the name Gorbachev has given to his program of economic renewal.

ruble   The Soviet currency, which, because it is nonconvertible, is worthless outside the Soviet Union and other Communist states.

Sobory   The local land councils that officially shared power with the czars and the council of boyars.

soviets   The local cells of workers formed by the Bolsheviks before the 1917 Revolution and retained afterward.

ukaz   An official edict handed down by the czar.

Zemsky Sobor   Translated as "the assembly of the country," it was composed of the landowners and elected Ivan IV the first czar in 1549. It is also referred to as "the Sobor."

INDEX

PICTURE CREDITS

AP/Wide World Photos: pp. 35, 70, 122; © 1991 ARS, NY/ADAGP: p. 88; Art Resource, NY: pp. 48, 55, 57, 59; Art Resource/Beniaminson: p. 39; The Bettmann Archive: pp. 41, 44, 64, 68, 69 (bottom); Ben Cohen: p. 28; Courtesy of Marcia Cohen: p. 34; Library of Congress: pp. 32, 46, 52, 60, 61, 72, 79; Reuters/Bettmann Archive: pp. 2, 16, 19, 20, 42, 92, 94, 96, 97, 100, 104, 106, 108, 115, 118, 121; Scala/Art Resource, NY: pp. 81–87; Donna Sinisgalli: pp. 6–7; Sovfoto: pp. 22, 24, 26, 29, 120; Sygma Photos: cover; Tass from Sovfoto: p. 112; UPI/Bettmann Archive: pp. 69 (top), 90, 114